THE GNOSTICS,

THE NEW VERSIONS

and

THE DEITY OF CHRIST

By
Jay P. Green, Sr.

Published by
Sovereign Grace Publishers
Lafayette, Indiana 47903
1994

ISBN 1-878442-71-6

Verses quoted are from the following editions:

Display Verses are from The Interlinear Hebrew-Greek-English Bible, Copyright © 1980, 1981, 1983, Second Revised Edition, © 1984, by Jay P. Green, Sr.

KJV - The King James Version, Authorised Version, Copyright © 1769 by The Cambridge University Press

LITV - A Literal Translation of the Bible, Copyright © 1985, by Jay P. Green, Sr.

MKJV - The Modern King James Version of the Holy Bible, Copyright © 1962, 1990, 1992, 1993 by Jay P. Green, Sr.

NKJV - The New King James Version, Copyright © 1980, 1982 by Thomas Nelson, Inc.

NIV - The New International Version, Copyright © 1973, 1978, 1984 by International Bible Society

NASB - The New American Standard Bible, Copyright © 1960, 1962, 1963, 1968, 1971, 1972, 1973, 1975, 1977, The Lockman Foundation

NRSV - The New Revised Standard Version Bible, Copyright © 1989 by the Division of Christian Education of the National Council of Churches of Christ

REB - The Revised English Bible, Copyright © 1989 by Oxford University Press and Cambridge University Press

GNB - Good News for Modern Man, Copyright © 1966, 1971 by The American Bible Society

NAB - The New American Bible, Copyright © 1990 by The Oxford University Press, Inc.

ERV - The New Testament Easy-to-Read Version, Copyright © 1987 by World Bible Translation Center, Inc.

CEV - Comtemporary English Version New Testament, Psalms and Proverbs, Copyright © 1991, 1992, by The American Bible Society

MARS - The Interlinear Greek-English New Testament, Copyright © 1958, as the Literal English Translation, by Samuel Bagster and Sons, Ltd.

JWB - The Kingdom Interlinear Translation of the Greek Scriptures, copyright © 1969 by Watch Tower Bible & Tract Society of Pennsylvania

Published by Sovereign Grace Publishers
P.O. Box 4998
Lafayette, Indiana 47903, U.S.A.

Printed in the United States of America

Table of Contents

PREFACE

The single most distinctive difference between Christianity and all other salvation systems is this, that only Christianity has a Savior who saves without any input from the will or works of mankind. Not only was, and is, Christ Jesus holy, harmless, and undefiled, but He is co-equal God, one in essence with the other Persons in the Trinity. Christ as God Almighty, Jehovah of hosts, the great I AM, ever-existent, eternal, omnipotent, omniscient, immutable, alone is able to save men to the uttermost without any help from sinners. All the religions of the world preach a salvation by works. They cannot provide, nor even imagine, such a Savior as Christ Jesus, being wholly Divine and wholly human.

The full-orbed portrayal of Christ cannot be seen outside of the Holy Scriptures. It is there that we learn that He possesses all the attributes of God, that He retained those attributes even when He was joined with flesh and became the Godman. It is in the Scriptures that we are taught that Christ is the Way, the Truth, and the Life, and that it is only through Him, His righteousness, His sacrificial death for the specific persons predestinated to eternal life, and His bodily resurrection into Heaven to sit at the right hand of God the Father as intercessor for His elect people that we can be saved.

"All Scripture is God-breathed, and is profitable for reproof, for correction, for instruction in righteousness, that the man of God may be perfect, fully furnished for every good work" (2 Tim. 3:16).

Ever since the last God-breathed words of the Scriptures were written by the apostle John as he was *"being borne along by the Holy Spirit"* (2 Peter 1:21), Satan, his army of demons, and the ungodly men who are taken captive at his will (2 Tim. 2:26), have worked diligently to corrupt and adulterate God's Word. Among the most evil opponents of the Gospel of Jesus Christ have been the Gnostics. In the early centuries after the death of Christ the life and death struggle to maintain the purity of the Scriptures was at its fiercest. It was open

v

knowledge that manuscripts were being altered, and that in Egypt the Gnostics had become such a dominant force that the manuscripts executed in Egypt were to be suspected.

WHY DID THE GNOSTICS OPPOSE THE DEITY OF CHRIST?

To understand why the Gnostics in particular, and all unredeemed men in general, adamantly seek to discredit the deity of Christ, one needs to know what they believed:

1. The Gnostics claimed to possess a higher knowledge than is contained in Christianity.
2. They believed themselves to be spirit, while all other people were soul and body.
3. They believed that matter was evil.
4. Their views produced sensuality, or asceticism.
5. They rejected the Old Testament, and its God, Jehovah.
6. They allegorized all the teachings of Scripture in order to achieve a strange conformity between Gnosticism and Christianity.
7. They invented a creator who was a begotten creature, to whom they gave various names, the Demiurge, the Artificer, etc. They were willing for Christ to be a creator as long as it was agreed that He was an inferior god.
8. They claimed that Christ's body was an illusion, a fantasy.

Therefore, the Gnostics focused on destroying the image of Christ as co-equal God. How well they have succeeded in their evil design to dethrone Christ in the Scriptures may be seen in a study of the various Greek manuscripts executed in Egypt. Though Satan planned it, and the Gnostics executed his plan, it is doubtful that either of them could have dreamed of a day when those same adulterated, corrupted manuscripts would be elevated to such a height that Bible version after Bible version would appear with their falsified Scriptures intact in many places of the new versions of the twentieth century. But such is the case today.

NINE OF THE NEW VERSIONS HAVE ADOPTED GNOSTIC CORRUPTIONS

Upon studying certain portions of the Scriptures, the author was appalled, thoroughly shocked, when it was found that the NASB and NIV, supposedly 'conservative' translations, had eliminated such a noted testimony to the Deity of Christ as *God manifest in the flesh*. Other new versions were searched to see if they did this also. The following pages reveal the more extensive studies that were made to discover how the new versions treat the deity of Christ.

Such notable Gnostic corruptions as that in Matthew 19:16-19, where the Scriptures were altered to make Christ deny His own goodness, have been resurrected and inserted into nine of the new versions. And this in spite of the fact that the many words the new versions have cast out of Matthew appear intact in Mark 10:17, 18 and Luke 18:18, 19. This, of course, puts a direct contradiction within the new versions. Further study turned up Ebionite, Manachean, and other heretical beliefs being reinserted into new versions. Among other things, the virgin birth, the sinlessness, the omnipresence, and other essential doctrines testifying to Christ as God have been changed or denied in the new versions.

God's words are precious, and especially precious are those verses which assure us that Christ is co-equal God, ever-existing, without beginning or end. Because of this, it is important that every lover of Christ and His Word must be alerted to what is being done in the new versions, each new one being more corrupt than those that went before. And having been informed, it is essential that all true believers spread the message that the Scriptures are being stolen away from them under the guise of a 'new' version which promises to be more readable, more stylish, etc. The words may be different, but the evil doctrines seen in these new versions are as old as Satan himself. For He has ever been efficient in moving unbelieving men and women to deny the deity of Christ, and to assert that it is by their good will and works that they will be saved.

For the cause of God and Truth, for the love of our Savior God, Jesus Christ, go forth and make known the message of this book.

THE GNOSTICS,
THE NEW VERSIONS
and
THE DEITY OF CHRIST
by Jay P. Green, Sr.

A common feature of virtually all the new Bible versions is seen in their treatment of those Scriptures which attest to the deity of Jesus Christ. The common feature is a weakening of the doctrine that declares that Christ is co-equal with God the Father and God the Holy Spirit, that He was of the same essence, having the same attributes, as the other two Persons in the Godhead.

Very early, even before the death of the apostle John, Cerinthus the Gnostic prominently denied the deity of Christ. While God the Spirit closely guided the servants of God to carefully preserve the original manuscripts, and to disseminate copies throughout the habitable world, Satan, the rejected evil spirit, directed his human dupes to corrupt and adulterate the Word of God. Gnostic sects were reared up and were vicious in their attempt to discredit Jesus Christ, claiming Him to be a created being, only a superman, not God. Adulterated manuscripts were created to serve their purposes, some, practically eliminating the Old Testament.

Among these was Marcion, an early Gnostic (c. 150 A.D.), who rejected the OT, and slashed the NT to bits as well. But despite all this evil activity, only in Egypt were the Gnostics able to dominate. In this they were aided immensely by the intellect and talent of Origen (c. 185-254 A.D.), an early Gnostic who specialized in textual criticism, but he was somewhat more honest than many textual critics since. For instance, Origen scoffed at many of the corruptions which are now being inserted into the new versions (such as an eclipse at Passover time, Luke 22:45). But Origen did not believe in the deity of Jesus Christ in the sense that Christ was a co-equal Person in the Trinity, and so his efforts were often bent toward depicting our Lord as a man created for the purpose of creating the world, and to seminally have within Him all things to come. For instance Origen wrote that Christ was "inferior to the Father who is the God (*o theos*). The Son is divine in a derivative sense, for he gains his deity by communication from the Father, 'the only true God' (John 17:3), who is preeminent as the single source or foundation of deity" [quoted from *Johannem*, 10:37 in *Jesus as God*, by Murray J. Harris, Grand Rapids, Baker Book House, 1990].

Today the fierce battle to maintain the purity and integrity of the Scriptures is crucial. For among 'theologians' there is a falling away from the stance of the early Christians, who risked their lives and property to maintain the co-equal deity of Jesus Christ, one in essence with the Father and the Holy Spirit. Every lover of Jesus Christ must also love and reverence the Scriptures that teach us who He is and what He did in order to obtain remission for his or her sins (that He did this by living a sinless life and dying a perfect sacrifice). As soldiers of the Cross we cannot lie down on the job, leaving the defense of God's Word to others. To arm the saints for the battle, we present here some key Scripture verses which attest to the Godhead of Jesus Christ, He being perfect God and perfect Man, the only One who could obtain full satisfaction for all the sins of His elect people.

In today's Bible market, the sincere Christian is faced with this question: Do you want to know exactly what God has written for your spiritual wellbeing, or, Do you want to know what the translators of today's versions say is the meaning of the words God wrote for your spiritual wellbeing? In brief, it comes down to this: Do you want to read a version of the Bible with words that God actually wrote, or, Are you satisfied to read a version that contains God's word masticated, swallowed, and regurgitated by mere men?

To aid the Christian in deciding on which version reports the words that God exactly wrote, this book presents what the new versions have recorded as being God's Word. Note how the new versions treat the deity of Christ, how many times the addition and subtraction of words leave them denying the Godhood of Christ Jesus.

LEGEND

[ ] All words bracketed [ ] do not accurately translate the original words.

☒ When the words have been left untranslated, or are inaccurately translated, the place is marked by the sign ☒ (in those cases where the versions are so lacking in conformity to the original Greek, we may have failed to indicate all the words not translated. Those having The Interlinear Bible can see which words correctly translate the original words of the vast majority of extant Hebrew and Greek manuscripts as collected into the Masoretic and Received Texts.

In the OT where the capitalized LORD or GOD appear, the original has Jehovah. Above each verse we have added the Greek of the Received Text, and the Hebrew of the Masoretic Text, as it appears in The Interlinear Hebrew-Greek-English Bible.

INITIALED REFERENCES:

MKJV = *The Modern King James Version*

NKJV = *The New King James Version*

LITV = *The Literal Translation of the Bible*

MARSH = *Marshall's Interlinear Greek-English New Testament*

ERV = *The Easy Reading Version*

NIV = *The New International Version*

NASB = *The New American Standard Bible*

NRSV = *The New Revised Standard Version*

REB = *The Revised English Bible*

GNB = *The Good News Bible* (Today's English Version)

NAB = *The New American Bible* (Roman Catholic Version)

CEV = *The Contemporary English Version*

JWV = *The Kingdom Interlinear Translation* (The Greek compiled by Westcott and Hort, adopted by the Jehovah's Witnesses because it so fully supports their belief that Christ was a created Being)

3

Other abbreviations which appear in this treatise are:

OT = Old Testament
NT = New Testament
NU = the Nestle^{26}\UBS^3 Greek
WH = Westcott and Hort's choices

MANUSCRIPTS:

p^{45}, p^{46} = Chester Beatty (both c. 200 A.D.)
p^{47} = Chester Beatty (c. 250 A.D.)
p^{66} = Bodmer (c. 200 A.D.)
p^{72} = (c. 250 A.D.)
p^{74} = Bodmer (c. 650 A.D.)
p^{75} = Bodmer (c. 200 A.D.).
Aleph = *Sinaiticus* (c. 375 A.D.)
A = *Alexandrinus* (c. 400 A.D.)
B = *Vaticanus* (c. 325 A.D.)
C = *Ephraim* (c. 450 A.D.)
D = *Bezae (c. 350 - 550* A.D.), or, *Clarimontanus* (c. 550 A.D.)
F = *Aupensis* (c. 850 A.D.)
G = *Boernarianus* (c. 850 A.D.)
L = *Regius* (c. 750 A.D.)
W = *Washington* (c. 400 A.D.)
Theta = *Voridethe* (c. 850 A.D.)
Uncials = Greek mss. written in capital letters with no break between words.
Cursives = Greek mss. written in script, dating from the ninth century
    forward.

OBSERVE THE FOLLOWING TWENTY-ONE NEW VERSION TEACHINGS REGARDING THE GODHOOD OF CHRIST:

1. Words that identify Christ as God are stolen away. And if these omissions are not enough, bogus words are slipped into the text. These mud links in the chain of proofs of Christ's deity tend to enhance the idea that Christ is a created Being. For this reason, the Mormons, Jehovah's Witnesses, Unitarians, and other adversaries of Christ are encouraged in their disobedience.

2. The Bible's witness to the self-sufficient power of Christ to save, sustain, guide, and intercede is weakened by the changes in the new versions. Rather than presenting Christ as a Savior suffering and dying for His own elect people, verse after verse of the new versions dilute His work of salvation. Out and out universal salvation is taught in many verses.

3. Philippians 3:20, 21 in these new versions present Christ as one who must be enabled in order to exert power and subdue opposition. For example, in these verses alone the NASB adds 14 words which are not translations of the Greek they were supposed to translate, and not one of those 14 words are italicized in the NASB!

4. In John 3:13, the Bible's only specific witness to the omnipresence of our Savior God, Christ, while on earth is completely removed in the major new versions, and this on very slight evidence.

5. By ignoring the connection expressed in Galatians 3:16 (with such verses as Gen. 21:12), the new versions destroy an important fulfillment of prophecy, the coming of Christ as the Promised Seed. And, incidentally, this verse testifies to the extreme care taken to preserve not only the message of the Hebrew Scriptures, but even the very grammatical construction. The singular word, Seed, was preserved for 3500 years until the recent plethora of new versions change seed to other words, some of them plurals.

6. The character of the new version approach to Christ's deity can be plainly seen in their wording of Hebrews 1:3. There they present Him as a copy, an imprint, a representation, etc., rather than "the express image of God's essence."

7. In John 4:26; 8:24, 58; 18:5, 6, 8; etc. words are added, or capitalization withheld, to hide Christ's identification of Himself as the Divine I AM, the self-existing, eternal God.

8. In Hebrews 1:8; Proverbs 8:22; Micah 5:2 the new versions make Christ to be a created Being, one with a beginning. But Christ is God, and God has no beginning.

9. Deceitful footnotes often throw doubt on the words of the text, such as may be found at Mark 1:1; Romans 9:5, etc. Worse, yet, in other places when words that witness to the Godhead of Christ are removed from the text, seldom is there a footnote to call attention to it. And when there is a footnote purporting to give evidence for the change, a false impression is often given by an incomplete presentation of the facts.

5

10. In Philippians 2:5-7, Christ is misrepresented as making Himself nothing (ERV. NIV), and the REB actually says that He did not claim equality with God. Plain contradictions between passages in the same version abound in these new versions, as well as contradictions between versions.

11. In Psalm 110:3, Christ's power to make His people willing in the day of His power is completely removed in the new versions.

12. In Isaiah 8:14, Romans 9:33, 1 Peter 2:8 the new versions present the lie that Christ causes men to fall and stumble.

13. In Matthew 19:17-19, the new versions present Christ as denying His own goodness, breathing new life into a Gnostic heresy of the second century. And this is done in the face of Mark 10:7, 8; Luke 18:18, 19 which present the same words that these new versionists cast out of Matthew 19. Consistency and logic are jewels apparently unknown to these cultic followers of Codex B and a handful of other Egyptian manuscripts.

14. In 1 Timothy 3:16 the testimony to Christ as "God manifest in the flesh" is summarily dismissed on the basis of ONE corrupt manuscript (Aleph), 5 cursives, and 1 version. As a cover up they unite in presenting an imaginary hymn as the origin of the verse, a hymn which does not credit Christ with being God. These new versionists preferred a self-concocted myth to the evidence supporting "God manifest in the flesh." The massive evidence to the contrary is simply ignored, including dozens of quotations from the early patristic fathers, all the other versions, and every other uncial manuscript except D.

15. By bracketing, doubting footnotes, or plain removal, the only two explicit references to the bodily resurrection of Christ are rejected from the new versions. Can a book be called a Bible without the Ascension of Christ being reported in it?

16. By removing Firstborn from Matthew 1:25, and by presenting Joseph as the father of Jesus in Luke 2:33, His virgin birth is left open to question. Luke 2:33 is also made even to contradict Luke's account of the Holy Spirit's fathering of Jesus.

17. By removing a single little Greek word (*eike - without a cause*) the new versions make Christ subject to, liable to judgment. This is tantamount to making Him a sinner, for only sinners are liable to judgment. Then in John 7:8, again they leave out a single word (yet - *oupo*), and report Jesus as saying that He will not go up to the Feast. Then they go on to report that He did go up to the feast. So in those versions that leave out the word yet, they are presenting Jesus as telling a lie.

18. The scriptural testimony to the purpose and fulfillment of the work of Christ as Savior is turned on its head by the new versions in many verses of the NT, thereby nullifying the extensive testimony of the manuscripts that He suffered for a certain group (us - 1 Pet. 2:21; 4:1), was sacrificed for them (1 Cor. 5:7), died to redeem them and bring them to God (1 Peter 3:18; Heb. 2:9); in order that they might believe

into Him (John 6:47); that they might become co-heirs of God with Him (Rom 8:17; Gal. 4:17).

19. The new versions change the "judgment seat of Christ" to 'judgment seat of God' in Rom. 14:10 on very poor evidence. Yet in 1 Cor. 5:10, they have "judgment seat of Christ"

20. By removing the words "Man" and "the Lord," the Gnostics destroyed the witness of 1 Cor. 15:47,48 to the eternal sonship of Christ. The new versions completely accept this stealing away of three words that are needed to balance the argument, and to testify to the fact that the Lord Jesus Christ came down from Heaven to save His people.

21. Those new versions which freely add words that do not translate the original languages, while at the same time passing over words in the text without translating them, they have produced a version from which **the doctrine of plenary and verbal inspiration cannot be taught.** The Bible writers were "borne along by [the] Holy Spirit" (2 Pet. 1:21) therfore it is written that the Scriptures are God-breathed (2 Tim. 3:16), and therefore infallible or inerrant. This assures us that the inspiration of the Bible is plenary (all of it complete, not partial, not lacking in any way), and verbal (involving every word of it, NOT merely the ideas or thoughts that rise from them). Only such a view of inspiration regards the entire Bible as the Word of God. Thought is expressed only in words, and only by controlling the exact words written could the Holy Spirit convey precisely the thought that He intended to convey. "Anything less than the verbal and plenary inspiration of the Bible yields a Bible which is a mixture of Divine truth and human error" (Johannes Vos, Bible article in *The Classic Bible Dictionary*, Sovereign Grace Trust Fund, 1989).

The Lord Jesus said that "the Scriptures cannot be broken" (John 10:35). It is our belief that the "dynamic equivalent" approach to the translation of the Scriptures is guilty of breaking up the Scriptures. And this in turn is based on the notion that "moving words of human wisdom" (1 Cor. 2:6, 7, 13) could improve upon the words that God breathed out.

Surely it can be said with confidence that the versions that add and subtract from the word written in the original languages have violated the following Scriptures:

"You shall not add to the word which I command you, nor take from it" (Deuteronomy 4:2a).

"Every word of God is tested; He [is] a shield to [those] seeking refuge in Him. Do not add to His words, lest He reprove you and you be found a liar" (Proverbs 30:5, 6).

"For I testify together with everyone hearing the words of the prophecy of this Book: If anyone will add to these things, God will add on him the plagues having been written in this Book. And if anyone takes away from the words of [the] Book of this prophecy, God will take away his part from [the] Book of Life, and out of the holy city, and of the things having been written in this Book" (Revelation 22:18, 19).

7

THE FIRST TARGET OF THE ADULTERATORS IS THE WORD ITSELF

First, it should be seen that those seeking to dilute, delete, adulterate, and corrupt the God-breathed words of the Scriptures must convince us that God has not preserved the original words which He spoke through the prophets and apostles. In this first verse you will see that only the KJV, MKJV, NKJV, LITV have truly translated the Hebrew. The rest have rejected the idea that God preserves His Word:

THE NEW VERSIONS AND THE WORD OF GOD

Jeremiah 23:30

30 — from / each / man / My / .words / who / steal / Jehovah says / the / .prophets / against / ,behold / (am) I / ,fore / There-

31 — their / tongue / take who / the / Jehovah says / the / .prophets / against / am I / his / :neighbor

KJV: ....Therefore, behold, I [am] against the prophets, saith the Lord, that steal my words every one from his neighbour.

LITV: ....Therefore, behold! I [am] against the prophets, says Jehovah, who steal My words, each man from his neighbor.

MKJV: ......So says the LORD, Behold! I [am] against the prophets who steal My words each man from his neighbor.

ERV: ...."So ☒ ☒ ☒, ☒ I [am] against the [false] prophets." [This message is from] the Lord. [These prophets keep] stealing my words ☒ ☒ from ☒ ☒ one another."

NIV: ....Therefore, declares the LORD, "I [am] against the prophets who steal ☒ ☒ ☒ from one another words [supposedly] from [me]."

NASB: ...."Therefore, behold, I [am] against the prophets, declares the LORD, who steal my words ☒ ☒ from ☒ ☒ [each] other."

REB: ....Therefore I [am] against those prophets, [the impostors] who steal my words ☒ ☒ from the other[s]

NAB: ....Therefore I [am] against the prophets, says the LORD, who steal my words ☒ ☒ from [each] other.

ANALYSIS 1: Since only the KJV, LITV, MKJV and NASB of the new versions quoted here italicize words not in the original Hebrew, we have bracketed the words that are not backed by the Hebrew, and also have marked with the sign ☒ the places where the Hebrew words are not translated, or are mistranslated. The ERV adds many words, but they leave intact the fact that the LORD (Jehovah) is against the prophets who steal His words. But the NIV completely misrepresents the key Hebrew words. In their usual boldness they add an interpretation completely foreign to what God has written through Jeremiah. For instead of identifying the words as God's words that are being stolen, the NIV deletes My before words, and displaces words, putting it into the last phrase, adding a bogus word and rearranges the last phrase from *"who steal My words each from his neighbor"* to *"who steal from one another words supposedly from me ."*

The other new versions at least keep intact the fact that they were God's words being stolen. But the NIV would mislead the reader into thinking that the stolen words were only supposedly God's words. In this instance the NIV manages to put itself into the position of one who is stealing God's words from His lambs, and putting in their own words instead.

What did God say? Here it is from the Jewish Publication Society translation: "Therefore, behold, I am against the prophets, says the LORD, that steal My words [every one] from his neighbor."

ANALYSIS 2: Since saving faith is based on God's Word written, when a version deliberately mistranslates, or simply refuses to translate, the original language in which the Scriptures are written, it should be obvious to all that one cannot put his faith in that version.

Keep firmly in mind the fact that ALL these versions claim to be translating the Masoretic Text of the Old Testament.

Deuteronomy 8:3b

KJV: ....that he might make thee know that man doth not live by bread only, but by every word that proceedeth out of the mouth of the Lord doth man live.

MKJV: ......so that He might make you know that man shall not live by bread alone. But man shall live by every word that comes out of the mouth of the LORD.

ERV: ....[Why did the Lord do these things? Because he [wanted] you to know that ⊠ ⊠ [it is] not [just] bread [that keeps people alive. People's lives depend on what the Lord says.]

NIV: ....⊠ ⊠ [to teach] ⊠ ⊠ ⊠ you ⊠ that man [does] not live [on] bread alone but ⊠ ⊠ ⊠ ⊠ [on] every word that comes from the mouth of the LORD.

NASB: ...... that He might make you [understand] that man does not live by bread alone, but man shall live by everything that proceeds out of the mouth of the LORD.

ANALYSIS: Since all the versions generally agree that man shall live by every word (or every thing) that comes out of the mouth of God, they

9

cannot defend their additions to God's words, nor their subtractions from God's words (by not translating some of the words). There is not a word in the Holy Scriptures that will lead anyone to pretend that God gives them license to present as His words whatever words a translator may decide to add. Nor will there be found any scriptural statement which will permit a translator to substitute, or simply to ignore, a word or words, and thereby misrepresent what the original language says.

Consider the least inaccurate of the new version corrupters, the NASB. They claim in their prefatory remarks: "Italics are used in the text to indicate words which are not found in the original Hebrew or Greek but implied by it." They are saying that they italicize words that are not reflected in the original language. Yet they add and do not italicize hundreds of words which are not in accordance with the original language they supposedly are translating. EXAMPLE: 1 Cor. 11:16, in which the original Greek says: "But if any seems to be contentious, we do not have any such custom, neither the churches of God."

But the NASB (also the NIV, NRSV and GNB) mistranslates *toianten* (#5108) by reading: "we have no other practice (custom)." So, as Gordon Clark points out in his commentary, these versions are making God to say words that are directly opposite to what He DID say. Yet the NASB does NOT italicize other, though *toianten* cannot be translated as other.

The others, never allowing the reader to know when they add or subtract a word, must be regarded as having no authenticity when they claim their version is a Holy Bible, or God's Word. Instead of entitling their production as The Holy Bible, they would more truthfully entitle their versions as The Adulterated Scriptures (2 Cor. 2:17).

Luke 4:4

```
         611      2424    4314    846      3004       1125      3754
    4  και ἀπεκρίθη Ἰησοῦς πρός αὐτόν, λέγων, Γέγραπται ὅτι
       And made answer  Jesus   to      him.     saying. It has been written,
       3756/1909/740  3441   2198            444        235/1909/3956
       Οὐκ ἐπ' ἄρτῳ μόνῳ ζήσεται ὁ ἄνθρωπος, ἀλλ' ἐπὶ παντὶ
       Not on  bread  only  shall live        man.     .  but  on  every
         4487    2316        321        846       1228      1519   3735
    5  ῥήματι Θεοῦ. και ἀναγαγών αὐτόν ὁ διάβολος εἰς ὄρος
       word  of God. And leading up   Him    the    Devil    into a mount
```

KJV: ....And Jesus answered him, saying, It is written, That man shall not live [by] bread alone, but by every word of God.

MKJV: .....And Jesus answered him, saying, It is written that "Man shall not live [by] bread alone, but on every word of God."

ERV: ....☒ Jesus answered ☒, "It is written [in the Scriptures]: ["It is not just bread that keeps people alive."] ☒ ☒ ☒ ☒ ☒ ☒

NIV: ....☒ Jesus answered ☒, "It is written: Man [does not] live [on] bread alone." ☒ ☒ ☒ ☒ ☒ ☒

NASB: ......And Jesus answered ☒ , ☒ [and said], It is written, Man shall not live on bread alone ☒ ☒ ☒ ☒ ☒ ☒

NRSV: ......☒ Jesus answered him, It is written, [One does] not live by bread alone ☒ ☒ ☒ ☒ ☒ ☒

REB: .... ☒ Jesus answered ☒ , [Scripture says], Man [is] not [to] live on bread alone ☒ ☒ ☒ ☒ ☒ ☒

ANALYSIS: The NAB, CEV, JWV all also omit the important words, "but on every word of God". Note that these words ARE in the Nestle[26]/UBS[3] in Matthew, but not in Luke. But 99% of the MSS. DO have those words in Luke 4:4.

Question: Was Matthew right in reporting what Jesus answered, or was Luke? Which one was being "borne along by the Holy Spirit" as they wrote? Silly questions? Yes, because the Holy Spirit is the Author of the Scriptures, speaking God's truth through the individual prophets and apostles. Here the very words of Jesus are being reported. Neither Matthew nor Luke were present to hear what Jesus said to the devil. Therefore, in this case, particularly, the Holy Spirit is the only witness, and the only reporter. Would He lead Luke to leave out these important words, especially since they are a quotation from Deut. 8:3b? In spite of the critics and the new versionists, we pray that you will not be led astray by their cultic-like adoration of the Egyptian MSS., Aleph (Sinaitic) and B (Vaticanus), here joined by other Egyptian mss., L, W (Washington) and some Latin mss.. Omissions abound in Aleph and B (nearly 7,000 omissions between them), so it is absurd to take the testimony of four mss. full of omissions as proof that their lack of certain words proves that the words in 2,000 other mss. are fraudulent.

Evidence the omitted words are Divine: A, D, ALL other uncials, all the cursives; the Gothic Version and most of the Syriac mss. do contain them.

What are the critics suggesting? Must we go through more than 2,000 witnesses to these words and bracket them as false? Consider this, Either, (1) scribes all over the habitable world deliberately falsified the Scriptures by adding these words; or, (2) some textual critic among the Gnostics (we would suggest Marcion, for He took his scissors to the Gospel of Luke) decided that Luke took these words from Matthew 4:4? It may be that the scribe of the ancestor of B sleepily omitted the words. A, an Egyptian ms. not much older than B and Aleph, has the words. Codex D, which has the most omissions among the uncials, did not omit these words.

ARE THE OLDEST EXTANT MANUSCRIPTS MORE APT TO HAVE THE PUREST TEXT?

Because of the many words confidently declared fraudulent by the modern critics and therefore left out of the new versions, it is important to consider at the outset whether the judgment of the critics is valid. Their argument is that the manuscripts nearest to the originals are more apt to be pure, just as the stream nearest to the source is apt to be most pure. When all pertinent facts are known, this proves to be untrue (if it is the Scriptures that are in view). Historical facts prove it untrue, since parties on both sides agree that some of the most vicious tampering with the biblical text occurred in the first three centuries after they were written. The proposition is also without force because (contrary to the critics' assumption), the Scriptures are not like any other book. They are Divine! Even before the NT was complete the apostles Paul and John warned that ravening wolves and antichrists would mount fierce opposition to the Word of Truth.

Dean John W. Burgon illustrates the difficulty by comparing a scrap of a manuscript containing Mark 10:17-31 found in the study of Clement of Alexandria (150 - c. 215 A.D.) with the Traditional Text, and also with the Westcott/Hort Greek. Burgon demonstrated that in 15 verses of Mark, within the 297 words in Clement's scrap containing Mark 10:17-31, if compared to the Received Text, 39 words were omitted; 11 added; 22, substituted; 27, transposed; 13, varied; and a phrase altered at least 8 times. He concluded this was a 38% error rate. When one objected to a comparison with the Received Text, Burgon then demonstrated that within these same 15 verses: Clement's text compared to the Westcott and Hort 'text' was found to have omitted 44 of the words Westcott/Hort chose as virtually being the original God-breathed words, 13 words were added; 23, substituted; 34 transposed; and 16 varied — an error rate of 44%! Burgon concludes: "It is impossible to produce a fouler exhibition of St. Mark 10-17-31 than is contained in a document full two centuries older than either Codex B or Aleph." And Clement is one of the most famous of the early fathers, the personal instructor of the even more famous Origen.

So much for the idea that the extant manuscripts are purer because they were executed closer to the originals. Clement's scrap from Mark no doubt was executed no more than fifty years after the death of John, and the closing of the NT canon. In that same second century one Caius wrote an accusation against his peers for putting out manuscripts which differed considerably from the manuscripts they were supposed to be copying, saying that when confronted with the originals, they could not deny their guilt.

THE NEW VERSIONS AND THE DEITY OF CHRIST
OMNIPOTENCE

Psalm 110:3

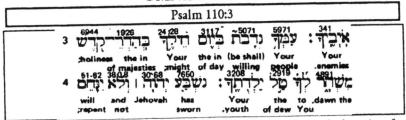

KJV: ....Thy people shall be willing in the day of thy power, in the beauties of holiness from the womb of the morning: thou hast the dew of thy youth.

MKJV: .....Your people [shall be] willing in the day of Your power, in the beauty of holiness from the womb of the morning; You have the dew of Your youth.

ERV: ....Your people [join you on] the day [you become king]. [You have had a holy beauty since birth]. [Now that blessing from your childhood is dawning into your new life as king].

NIV: ....Your [troops will be] willing on the day of [battle]. [Arrayed] in holy majesty, from the womb of the dawn you [will receive] the dew of your youth.

NASB: .....Thy people [will volunteer freely] in the day of Thy power; In holy array, from the womb of the dawn, Thy youth are to Thee as the dew.

NRSV: .....Your people ☒ ☒ [shall offer themselves willingly on] ☒ the day ☒ ☒ ☒ ☒ ☒ ☒ ☒ ☒ [you lead your forces on the holy mountains]. From the womb of the morning, ☒ ☒ [like] dew, ☒ your youth [will come to you].

NAB: ....[Yours is princely power] in the day of your [birth], in holy splendor, [before the daystar, like the] dew, [I have begotten you].

ANALYSIS: From ages past this verse has been used as proof that God the Son has an elect people, and that these are made willing on the predetermined day when His power is exerted to give them life, repentance, and faith. Now along come the new versionists to steal away this intent of the words. The NIV translates *'am* (5971) as troops (NRSV, troops) here, though in over 90% of the occurrences of the word they translate people. Why? If there was a military context, by a stretch they might translate troops, but in the context here it is the people of the Lord Jesus Christ, God the Son, that are in view. And further, the NIV translation of battle instead of power is wrong for the same reason. The basic meaning of the word (2428) is strength, power. Again, there is nothing military in the context which allows a translator to stretch the meaning to battle. So by this kind of misrepresentation the NIV robs the saints of a very important statement regarding the who and the how of salvation. The NAB barely touches the Hebrew at all, also destroying the precious promise that Christ's people will be willing in the day of His power.

The **NASB** and **NRSV** mislead the reader into thinking that the willingness of God's people is voluntary without the need for the exertion of God's power, the same power that works in us to believe: "and what is the surpassing greatness of His power toward us, the ones believing according to the working of His mighty strength which He worked in Christ [in] raising Him from [the] dead" (Eph. 1:18-20). The **NASB** and the **NRSV** also rework the last phrase from the original, which says, "To You the dew of Your youth."

THE NEW VERSIONS SAY THAT JESUS CAUSES MEN TO STUMBLE AND FALL

Isaiah 8:13

אֶת־יְהוָה צְבָאוֹת אֹתוֹ תַקְדִּישׁוּ וְהוּא מוֹרַאֲכֶם וְהוּא

		3372		6942		8636	3068	
and He	fear your (be will)	and He	,sanctify	Him	,hosts	Jehovah of		

מַעֲרִצְכֶם: וְהָיָה לְמִקְדָּשׁ וּלְאֶבֶן נֶגֶף וּלְצוּר מִכְשׁוֹל לִשְׁנֵי

	81...	/6307/6687	5063	68	4720	1961	8206
the to two	falling	a and of rock	stumb- line	a and of stone	a .sanctuary	He And become shall	.dread your

KJV: ....Sanctify the Lord of hosts himself; and [let] him [be] your fear, and [let] him [be] your dread

MKJV: .....Sanctify the LORD of hosts Himself, and [let] Him [be] your fear, and [let] Him [be] your dread.

ERV: .... ☒ The Lord [All-Powerful] ☒ ☒ ☒ ☒[is] the One you should be afraid of.] ☒ ☒ ☒ [He is the [One you should] respect. ☒ [He is] the ☒ ☒ [One you should] fear.

NIV: .... ☒ The LORD [Almighty is] the ☒ ☒ ☒ ☒ [one you should] ☒ ☒ fear, and he [is the one you are to] ☒ dread

NASB: ...... ☒ [It is] the LORD of hosts [whom you should regard as] holy. And He [shall be] your fear. And He [shall be] your dread.

NRSV: ..... ☒ [But] the LORD of hosts, him [you shall regard as holy]; [let] him [be] your fear, and [let] him [be] your dread.

NOTE: ....Not one of the bracketed words are italicized by the **NASB**. The Hebrew is: "Jehovah of hosts, sanctify Him, and He your fear, and He your dread." By this it is easily discerned that it is not the object of these new versions to merely translate the original, but instead they are set up as **commentaries parading under the name of Scriptures.** Note the **NIV**'s decision to report *Jehovah of hosts* as *the LORD [Almighty]*.

Isaiah 8:14

מַעֲרִצְכֶם: וְהָיָה לְמִקְדָּשׁ וּלְאֶבֶן נֶגֶף וּלְצוּר מִכְשׁוֹל לִשְׁנֵי

	81...	/6307/6687	5063	68	4720	1961	8206
the to two	falling	a and of rock	stumb- ling	a and of stone	a .sanctuary	He And become shall	.dread your

בָּתֵּי יִשְׂרָאֵל לְפַח וּלְמוֹקֵשׁ לְיוֹשֵׁב יְרוּשָׁלָ֑͏ִם: וְכָשְׁלוּ בָם

	3782	133 89	3427	141 70	6341	34 78	1004
among shall And them stumble	.Jerusalem	the to of dweller	a and snare	a for ___ trap	,Israel ___	houses of ___	

KJV: ....And he shall be for a sanctuary; but for a stone of stumbling and for a rock of offence to both the houses of Israel, for a gin and for a snare to the inhabitants of Jerusalem.

MKJV: .....And He shall be a sanctuary for you, but for a stone of stumbling, and for a rock of falling, to both the houses of Israel, for a trap and for a snare to the people of Jerusalem.

ERV: .... ☒ ☒ ☒ ☒ ☒ ☒ ☒ [If] you [will respect the Lord and consider him holy, then] he will be [a safe place for you. But you don't respect him. So God is like] ☒ ☒ a rock ☒ ☒ [that you people] fall over. [He is a] ☒ ☒ ☒ rock ☒ ☒ [that makes the two families] of Israel stumble. [The Lord is] ☒ ☒ a trap [to catch all] ☒ ☒ ☒ ☒ ☒ the people of Jerusalem.

NIV: ....and he will be a sanctuary ☒ ☒ , but [for] both houses of Israel [he will be] a stone [that <u>causes men to] stumble and a rock [that makes them] fall. And for the people of Jerusalem [he will be] a trap and a snare.</u>

NASB: ..... Then He shall become a sanctuary ☒ ☒; But to both the houses of Israel, ☒ ☒ a stone [to strike] and a rock [to] stumble [over], [And] ☒ a snare and ☒ a trap ☒ [for] the inhabitants of Jerusalem.

NRSV: ..... ☒ He will become a sanctuary; ☒ ☒ a stone [one strikes against]; ☒ for both house of Israel [he will become] a rock [one] stumbles [over] — a trap and a snare for the inhabitants of Jerusalem.

NAB: ....Yet he shall be a ☒ ☒ ☒ [snare, an obstacle] and a stumbling stone ☒ ☒ ☒ ☒ ☒ to both the houses of Israel, ☒ a trap and a snare to those who dwell in Jerusalem.

ANALYSIS: Unrepentant sinners may find cause for glee when they read in the NIV, ERV, and others that it is Christ (*The Stone-of-stumbling and the Rock-of-offense*) that according to these new versionists "causes men to stumble and causes men to fall." That is a pure lie against the truth, and of course is not at all what the Hebrew words (5063 and 6697-5307) say. The proof is recorded in the NT, where these words are quoted three times as Stone of stumbling, Rock of offense.

The NIV and these others seize upon the fact that 5307 in the Hebrew *HIPH.* may be translated as <u>cause to fall</u>, but 5063 does not allow it. Also in Rom. 9:33 and 1 Pet. 2:7 they do the same thing, again misrepresenting Christ as One who causes men to stumble and fall.

The NT Greek words (4348 and 4625) both may be translated as a stumbling block, an obstacle over which men stumble and fall. But note carefully that the stumbling-block does NOT cause the falling, but the one stumbling and falling is to blame because he or she does not take heed to the way they are going. In the case of salvation, there is more than ample warning from the Scriptures that only Jesus Christ is "the Way, the Truth, and the Life." If they stumble over Him and fall, it is their own fault; Christ does not cause any to fall over Him, but on the contrary, He has fully made known the fact that He came "to seek and to save the lost." They "stumble at the word" (1 Pet. 2:8).

The NAB removes Christ from the verse altogether, destroying another precious promise, and this in spite of the fact that this verse is quoted twice in the NAB NT in quite different words than the words the NAB uses to eject Christ from this OT verse.

16

Romans 9:33

```
      3561      4350         1063      3037        4348         2631
33  νόμου.  προσέκοψαν γάρ τῷ λίθῳ τοῦ προσκόμματς, καθὼς
 of law.   they stumbled  For at the Stone-     of-stumbling,      even as
    1125         2400/5087/1722/ 4622   3037  4348
 γέγραπται,  Ἰδοὺ τίθημι ἐν Σιὼν λίθον προσκόμματος καὶ
 it was written:  Behold, I place in  Zion  a Stone- of-stumbling      and
    4073    4625              3956    4100     1909 846 3756 2617
 πέτραν σκανδάλου· καὶ πᾶς ὁ πιστεύων ἐπ᾽ αὐτῷ οὐ καται-
 a Rock-of-offense,  and everyone believing  on    Him not will be
 σχυνθήσεται.
 put to shame.
```

KJV: ....As it is written, Behold, I lay in Sion a stumblingstone and rock of offence: and whosoever believeth on him shall not be ashamed.

MKJV: .....as it is written, "Behold, I lay in Zion a Stumbling-stone and a Rock of offense, and everyone believing on Him shall not be put to shame."

ERV: ....☒ ☒ ☒ ☒ [The Scripture talks about that stone:] "Look, I put in Zion a [stone that will make people fall]. [It is a rock that will make people sin. But the person that trusts in that rock] will never be made ashamed."

NIV: ....As it is written: "See, I lay in Zion a [stone that causes men to stumble] and a rock [that makes them fall], and [the one who trusts in] him will never be put to shame."

NRSV: .....as it is written, "See, I am laying in Zion a stone [that will make people stumble], ☒ a rock [that will make them fall], and [whoever] believes in him will not be put to shame."

REB: ....☒ ☒ ☒ ☒ [mentioned in scripture]: [Here] I lay in Zion a stone to trip over, a rock to stumble against; but [he] who [has] faith in [it] will not be put to shame.

NAB: ....as it is written, "Behold, I am laying a stone in Zion [that will make people] stumble and a rock [that will make them] fall, and [whoever] believes in him shall not be put to shame.

ANALYSIS: See above on Isaiah 8:13, 14. Apparently the ERV translators have stumbled over the NIV, as they so often do copy the errors from that version. The ERV also takes heart from the worldly success of the NIV, seeing it as an encouragement to add many more words of their own to their version, and thus causing it to be a far more untrustworthy guide, one not worthy to be called a Holy Bible. Note that neither the NRSV nor the NAB report what they said in Isaiah 8:14, thereby having a contradiction within their versions. Also in 1 Pet. 2:6 the NAB and REB change whoever believes in him to whoever believes in it! In the NAB it is, "For it says in scripture: "Behold, I am laying a stone in Zion, a cornerstone, chosen and precious, and whoever believes in it shall not be put to shame."

17

7 καὶ ὁ πιστεύων ἐπ' αὐτῷ οὐ μὴ καταισχυνθῇ. ὑμῖν οὖν ἡ
and the (one) believing on   Him   not at all shall be shamed. To you, then, the
5092   4100   544   3037/3739/ 593
τιμὴ τοῖς πιστεύουσιν· ἀπειθοῦσι δέ, Λίθον ὃν ἀπεδοκί-
honor, those believing.   to disobeying ones, But a stone which rejected
3618   3778   1096 1519 2776   1137
μασαν οἱ οἰκοδομοῦντες. οὗτος ἐγενήθη εἰς κεφαλὴν γωνίας,
those   building.   This (One) came to be for Head of (the) corner,

KJV: ....Unto you therefore which believe [he is] precious: but unto them which
be disobedient, the stone which the builders disallowed, the same is
made the head of the corner,

MKJV: .....Therefore to you, those who believe, [is] the honor. But to those who
are disobedient, [He is the] Stone which the builders rejected — this
One became the Head of the corner,

ERV: ....☒ ☒ [That stone (Jesus) is worth much] ☒ ☒ to you [people] who
believe. But to [the people who] don't believe, he is: "[the] stone that
the builders [decided they did not want.] ☒ ☒ [That stone] became
the ☒ ☒ ☒ ☒ [most important stone]."

NIV: ....Now to you ☒ who believe, [this stone] is [precious]. But to those who
do not believe, [The] stone the builders rejected ☒ ☒ ☒ has become
the ☒ ☒ ☒ ☒ [capstone],

NASB: .....[The precious value], then, [is] to you who believe. But to those who
disbelieve, "The stone which the builders rejected, This became ☒ ☒
☒ the [very] corner [stone]"

NRSV: .....To you then who believe, [he is] precious; but for those who do not
believe, "[The] stone that the builders rejected ☒ has become the
[very] head of the corner."

NAB: ....Therefore [its value is for] you who have faith, but [for] those [without]
faith: "The stone which the builders rejected ☒ ☒ has become the
corner[stone]."

See Next Page

18

```
         3037    4348              4073  4625      3739   4360
8  καί, Λίθος προσκόμματος καί πέτρα σκανδάλου· οἱ προσ-
and,  a Stone · of · stumbling,    and  a Rock-    of-offense  to those
            3056           544         1519/3739      5087    5210
9  κόπτουσι τῷ λόγῳ ἀπειθοῦντες· εἰς ὃ καί ἐτέθησαν. ὑμεῖς
stumbling  at the  word   disobeying,  to which indeed they were  you
                                                      appointed.
```

KJV: ....And a stone of stumbling, and a rock of offence, [even to them] which
stumble at the word, being disobedient: whereunto also they were
appointed.

MKJV: .....and a Stone-of-stumbling and a Rock-of-offense to those disobeying,
who stumble at the word, to which they also were appointed.

ERV: ....[To people who] don't believe, [he is]: "a stone ☒ ☒ ☒ [that makes
people] stumble, ☒ a ☒ ☒ ☒ [stone that makes people] fall."
[People] stumble [because they don't obey what God says. This is what
God planned to happen to those people].

NIV: ....and, a stone [that causes men to] stumble and a rock [that makes them]
fall." [They stumble because they] disobey ☒ ☒ the [message] - ☒
which [is also what] they ☒ were [destined for].

NASB: .....and, "A Stone of stumbling and a Rock of offense;" for they stumble
☒ ☒ [because they are] disobedient [to] the word, [and] to this
[doom] they were also appointed.

NRSV: .....and a stone [that makes them] stumble, and a rock [that makes them
fall. They stumble [because they disobey] the word, ☒ ☒ [as] they ☒
were [destined] to [do].

NAB: ....and "A stone [that will make people] stumble, and a rock [that will make
them] fall. [They] stumble [by disobeying] the word, [as is their destiny].

ANALYSIS: By now should not one begin to question why it is that the NIV,
ERV, NRSV and NAB persist in making Christ to be the one who
causes sinners (disobedient unbelievers) to stumble and fall? Note also
that here and elsewhere the NIV does not like to translate logos as word,
especially when it can mean THE Word. Here they make it to be
message. But what is the message if it is not the Word? In Rev. 19:9 they
translate it as "the true word of God," but in other places they use
many substitute words which interfere with the reader's understanding
of what God is saying. Since there is no difference in text, this
denigration of Christ by learned Greek scholars seems to be without
excuse. A good example of substituting words that fail to reflect the
original is the use of destined, destiny in this verse. If they had used
predestined, it would have been closer. The word (#5087) has many
meanings, basically to put, place, lay, set out. It can also mean ordain.
The apostle Paul used it in 1 Thess. 5:9: "God has not appointed us to
wrath;" and again in 2 Tim. 1:11: "for which I was appointed a herald
and apostle, and a teacher of nations."

Destined has come to have a connection with the false concept, fate, as per
Webster: 1. To predetermine, as by fate.

Is it not bad enough to make Christ the cause of stumbling and falling among
unbelieving, disobedient men? Must they also make it their destiny,
thus giving the impression that it was their fate, not their sin, that
causes them to stumble and fall?

```
        3004  846 5102 1169 2075   3640              5119  1453
26  καὶ λέγει αὐτοῖς, Τί δειλοί ἐστε, ὀλιγόπιστοι ; τότε ἐγερθεὶς
And He says to them, Why afraid are you, little-faiths?      Then arising.
      2008        417                    2281            1096  1055
ἐπετίμησε τοῖς ἀνέμοις καὶ τῇ θαλάσσῃ, καὶ ἐγένετο γαλήνη
He rebuked the    wind    and the   sea,    and  there was a calm
```

KJV: ....And he saith unto them, Why are ye fearful, O ye of little faith? Then he arose, and rebuked the winds and the sea; and there was a [great] calm.

MKJV: .....And He said to them, Why are you afraid, little-faiths? Then He arose and rebuked the winds and the sea; and there was a [great] calm.

ERV: ....[Jesus] ☒ ☒ ☒ ☒ ☒ answered, "Why are you afraid? [You don't have enough faith]. Then [Jesus] stood and [gave a command to] the wind and the [waves]. ☒ ☒ ☒ ☒ ☒ ☒ [The wind stopped, and the [lake] became [very] calm."

NIV: ....☒ He ☒ ☒ ☒ replied, "[You of] little faith, why are you afraid?" Then he got up and rebuked the winds and the ☒ [waves], and [it] was [completely] calm.

NASB: .....And He said to them, Why are you timid, [you men of] little faith? Then He arose and rebuked the winds and the sea, and it became [perfectly] calm.

REB: ....☒ "Why are you [such cowards?]" he said ☒ ☒ [How] little faith [you have]! [With that] he got up and rebuked the wind and the sea, and there was a [dead] calm.

NAB: ....☒ "He said to them, Why are you [terrified, O you of] little faith?" Then he got up, ☒ rebuked the winds and the sea, and there was a [great] calm.

NRSV:...... And he said to them, "Why are you afraid, [you of] little faith?" And he got up and rebuked the winds and the sea; and there was a [dead] calm.

ANALYSIS: This demonstrates both the omnipotence of Jesus Christ and therefore His deity, for only God could control the winds and the sea.

Note that the NASB did not italicize any of the four added words (bracketed), contrary to their assurance in their preface that they italicized words that are not in the original. Note also that with one accord they add words before *little faiths*, and note that they all translated this word (*oligopistoi* - #3640) as a **singular** rather than a **plural, adding** *ye* in order to achieve the plural. It is not *little faith*, but *little faiths*.

20

Philippians 3:20, 21

KJV: ....For our conversation is in heaven; from whence also we look for the Saviour, the Lord Jesus Christ: Who shall change our vile body, that it may be fashioned like unto his glorious body, according to the working whereby he is able even to subdue all things unto himself.

MKJV: ......For our citizenship is in Heaven, from which also we are looking for the Savior, [the] Lord Jesus Christ, who will change our body of humiliation so that it may be fashioned like His glorious body, according to the working of His power, even to subdue all things to Himself.

ERV: .... ☒ [But] our ☒ [homeland] is in heaven. ☒ ☒ ☒ We are waiting for [our] Savior [to come from heaven. Our Savior is] the Lord Jesus Christ. ☒ [He] will change our [humble bodies] ☒ ☒ ☒ ☒ ☒ ☒ [and make them] like his [own] glorious body. ☒ ☒ ☒ ☒ [Christ can do this by] His power. [With that power Christ is able to rule all things.]

NIV: .... ☒ [But] our citizenship is in heaven. ☒ ☒ ☒ [And] we eagerly await ☒ [a] Savior [from there], [the] Lord Jesus Christ, who [by the] ☒ ☒ ☒ ☒ ☒ power [that enables him to bring] everything ☒ ☒ ☒ ☒ ☒ [under his control], will transform our [lowly bodies] so that ☒ ☒ ☒ ☒ [they will be] like his glorious body.

NASB: .....For our citizenship is in heaven, from which also we eagerly wait for a Savior, [the] Lord Jesus Christ; who will transform the body ☒ ☒ ☒ ☒ [of our humble state into conformity with the] body of His glory, ☒ ☒ ☒ [by the exertion] of [the] ☒ power [that He has] even to subject all things to Himself.

REB: .... ☒ ☒ ☒ ☒ ☒ [We by contrast are] citizens [of] heaven, and from ☒ ☒ [heaven] we expect [our] deliverer [to come], [the] Lord Jesus Christ. [He] will [transfigure] our [humble] [bodies and give them a form] like [that of] His glorious body, [by that] power [which enables him] ☒ to make all things subject to himself.

NRSV: .....[But] our citizenship is in heaven, and [it is from there that] we are expecting a Savior, [the] Lord Jesus Christ. [He] will transform the body of our humiliation that it may be conformed to the body of his

21

glory [by] the power [that] also [enables him] to make all things subject to himself.

ANALYSIS: Note the many words added and subtracted by the new versions, thus deceiving the reader as to what God said, and how He said it. For they are not observing the grammatical construction of God's words either. "according to the working of His ability to subject all things to Himself" is quite different from "[by the power that enables him to bring] everything [under his control]" (NIV). Or as the NRSV, [by the power that also enables] him to make all things subject to himself. The original Greek plainly shows that Jesus' power was within Himself as God. It was not an external power that was supplied to Him, enabling Him to subject all things to himself.

Note also that we have bracketed 16 words of the NASB because they do not properly reflect the Greek they chose to translate, yet not one of those words are italicized in the NASB!

John 6:21

```
          3004   846      1473  1510/3361 5399        2309    3767
20   σαν. ὁ δὲ λέγει αὐτοῖς, Ἐγώ εἰμι· μὴ φοβεῖσθε. ἠθελον ουν
21        He  But says to them.  I     AMI Do not fear. they desired Then
     2983   846   1519    4143          2112      4143     1096
     λαβεῖν αὐτὸν εἰς τὸ πλοῖον· καὶ εὐθέως τὸ πλοῖον ἐγένετο
     to take  Him   into the  boat;  and instantly the  boat    became
     1909    1093/1519/3739/ 5217
     ἐπὶ τῆς γῆς εἰς ἣν ὑπῆγον.
     at the land  tn which they were going.
```

KJV: ....Then they willingly received him into the ship: and immediately the ship was at the land whither they went.

MKJV: .....Then they willingly received Him into the boat. And immediately the boat was at the land where they were going.

ERV: ....☒ [After Jesus said this], ☒ ☒ [the followers were happy to] take ☒ [Jesus] into the boat. Then ☒ the boat ☒ ☒ [came to] the land [at the place] where they ☒ [wanted] to go.

NIV: ....Then they were willing to take him into the boat, and immediately the boat [reached the shore] where they were [heading].

NASB: .....They were willing therefore to receive Him into the boat, and immediately the boat was at the land to which they were going.

REB: ....[With that] they were [ready] to take him [on board] and immediately the boat [reached] the land they were [making for].

ANALYSIS: Most versions report this miracle, but there are few who realize what a miracle it was for Jesus to use His omnipotent power to simply set aside natural laws, and to cause the boat to immediately arrive at the land. Note that the ERV denies their readers the blessing of the miracle by dropping the word immediately.

OMNIPRESENCE

John 3:13

```
   1437 2036 5213      2032        4100            3762    305
13 ἐὰν εἴπω ὑμῖν τὰ ἐπουράνια, πιστεύσετε ; καὶ οὐδεὶς ἀναβέ-
If  I tell   you the heavenly things, will you believe? And no one has gone
        1519      3772      -1508- 1537       3772      2597
   βηκεν εἰς τὸν οὐρανόν, εἰ μὴ ὁ ἐκ τοῦ οὐρανοῦ καταβάς, ὁ
   up   into  —   Heaven   except He out of —  Heaven having  come the
   5207      444            5607/1722  3772          2531  down 3475
14 υἱὸς τοῦ ἀνθρώπου ὁ ὢν ἐν τῷ οὐρανῷ. καὶ καθὼς Μωσῆς
   Son   —   of man,  who Is in —  Heaven. And  as      Moses
```

KJV: ....And no man hath ascended up to heaven, but he that came down from heaven, [even] the Son of man which is in heaven.

LITV: ....And no one has gone up into Heaven except the [One] having come down out of Heaven, the Son of man who is in Heaven.

MKJV: .....And no one has ascended up to Heaven except He who came down from Heaven, the Son of man who is in Heaven.

ERV: .... ☒ The [only] one that has [ever] gone up to heaven [is] the [One] that came down from heaven - the Son of Man ☒ ☒ ☒ ☒.

NIV: ....☒ No one has ever gone into heaven except the one who came from heaven — the Son of man ☒ ☒ ☒ ☒,

NASB: .....And no one has ascended into heaven, but He who descended from heaven, [even] the Son of man ☒ ☒ ☒ ☒

REB: ....☒ No one has gone up into heaven except the [one] who came down from heaven, the Son of Man who is in Heaven.

NAB: ....☒ No one has gone up to heaven except the [one] who has come down from heaven, the Son of Man ☒ ☒ ☒ ☒.

NRSV: .....No one has ascended into heaven except the one who descended from heaven, the Son of Man ☒ ☒ ☒ ☒.

ANALYSIS: Only the KJV, LITV, MKJV, NKJV, REB follow the evidence: The *NIV, NASB, GNB, NRSV, CEV, JWV* follow the NU in omitting the words that testify to God the Son being both on earth and in Heaven while He was united to the flesh — and so was both God and Man.

What then is the manuscript and other evidence which causes our modern day critics and versionists to be so certain that **who is in Heaven** are spurious words, never having been breathed out by God the Spirit through the apostle John? Or to put it the other way, why are they confident when they say that these words were added by men?

Evidence for the Omission: MANUSCRIPTS: p66, p75, Aleph, B, L, T, and 33 = 2 papyri, 4 uncials, 1 cursive (*the first* 4 executed in Egypt at a time when the Gnostics dominated that nation; the latter 3 are late manuscripts executed by those who, like our modern critics, venerated Aleph and B).

VERSIONS: None FATHERS: 7

Evidence the words are Divine: MANUSCRIPTS: More than 1800, and that many more lectionaries = at *least* 99.5% of all manuscripts.

VERSIONS: 10 FATHERS: 38

23

The importance of these words cannot be emphasized too much. For if Jesus Christ was both God and Man, and if anyone should insist that He was not omnipresent (present everywhere at once), then it may be logically concluded that He could not be God. For all three Persons in the Godhead have their attributes forever, and to have one of those attributes missing would but prove that the Person who did not have one of them is not, and never was God. Because of this, it is easy to see why those who believed Jesus to be a created Being would corrupt manuscripts in order to take away this plain and clear witness to the deity of Jesus Christ, God the Son.

Because of its supreme importance, we repeat here Dean John W. Burgon's remarks from his treatise, *The Causes of the Corruption of the Traditional Text of the Holy Gospels, page 196*:

"Numerous as were the heresies of the first two or three centuries of the Christian era, they almost all agreed in this: that they involved a denial of the eternal Godhead of the Son of Man, denied that He is essentially very and eternal God"

"But the language of S. John was taken by those heretics who systematically maimed and misinterpreted that which belonged to the human nature of Christ. Relying on the present place [John 3:13], Apolinarius (310-390 A.D.) [Apolinarius taught that Jesus was God, but not perfectly human, having soul and body, but not spirit, His spirit being replaced by the *Logos*] is found to have read it without the final clause ["who is in Heaven"]. And certain of the orthodox (Greg. Naz., Greg. Nyssa, Epiphanius) while contending with Apolinarius were not unwilling to argue from the text so mutilated. Origen and the author of the Dialogus once, Eusebius twice, Cyril nineteen times, also leave off the words 'even the Son of Man' — from which it is insecurely gathered that those Fathers disallowed the clause which follows ["Who is in Heaven"]. On the other hand thirty-eight Fathers and ten versions maintained the genuineness of the words [who is in Heaven"]. It is found in every manuscript in the world except five (Aleph,B,L,T and one cursive, 33)" — [Now seven, for p66 and p75 had not been found in Burgon's time - Ed.].

[The words] "are recognized by *all* the Latin and *all* the Syriac versions; the Coptic; the Ethiopic [both Egyptian - Ed.], the Georgian; and the Armenian versions. They are recognized, quoted, or insisted on by Origen; Hippolytus; Athanasius; Didymus; Aphraates; Eustathius; Chrysostom; Theorodret; Cyril four times; Paulus Bishop of Emesa; Theodorus Mops.; Amphiochius; Severus; Theodorus Heracl.; Basilius Cil.; Cosmas; Damascene in 3 places, 4 other ancient Greek writers; and of the latins, Ambrose; Novatian; Hilary; Lucifer; Victorinus; Jerome; Cassian; Vigilius, Zeno; Marius; Maximus Atur; Capreolus; Augustine, etc. They are even acknowledged by Lachmann, Tregelles, and Tischendorf. Why then is there not so much as a hint from the Revisers [*English Revised Version*, 1881, and the new versions which follow them - Ed.] that there is such a mass of counter-evidence against the spurious reading of the favored uncials [Aleph, B]? Shame! Yes, shame on the learning which comes abroad only to perplex the weak, and to unsettle the doubting, and to mislead the blind! Shame on those occupying themselves with falsifying the inspired Greek text in countless places, and branding with suspicion some of the most precious utterances of the Spirit!"

"Let the Reader, with a map spread before him, survey the whereabouts of the several Versions above enumerated, and mentally assign each Father to his own approximate locality: then let him bear in mind that 995 of 1000 of the extant Manuscripts agree with those Fathers and Versions; and let him further recognize that those MSS. (executed at different dates in different countries) must severally represent independent remote originals, inasmuch as *no two of them are found to be quite alike.*"

"Next, let him consider that, *in all the Churches of the East*, these words from the earliest period were read as *part of the Gospel for the Thursday in Easter week*. That done, let him decide whether it is reasonable that two worshipers of Codex B [Westcott and Hort, 1881 A.D.] should attempt to thrust all this mass of ancient evidence clean out of sight by their peremptory sentence of exclusion 'Western and Syrian.'" Drs. Westcott and Hort inform us that '*the character of the attestation* marks' the clause ["who is in Heaven"] 'as a Western Gloss.' But the 'attestation' for retaining that clause — (*a*) Comes demonstrably from every quarter of ancient Christendom; (*b*) is more ancient (by 200 years) than the evidence for omitting it; — (*c*) is more numerous, in the proportion of 99 to 1; — (*d*) In point of respectability, stands absolutely alone. For since we have **proved** that Origen and Didymus, Epiphanius and Cyril, Ambrose and Jerome, **recognize** the words in dispute, of what possible textual significancy can it be if presently (*because it is sufficient for their purpose*) the same Fathers are observed to quote S. John 3:13 **no further than down to the words 'Son of Man'**? No person (least of all a professed Critic who adds to his learning a few grains of common sense and a little candor), can be misled by such a circumstance. Origen, Eusebius, Proclus, Ephraim Syrus, Jerome, Marius, when they are only insisting on the doctrinal sufficiency of the earlier words, naturally end their quotation at this place. The two Gregories (Naz. [ii. 87, 168] (Nyss. [Galland, vi 522]), writing against the Apolinarian heresy, of course quote the verse no further than Apolinarius himself was accustomed [for his heresy] to adduce it. . . ."

"About the *internal* evidence for the clause, nothing has been said; but *this* is simply overwhelming. We make our appeal to *Catholic Antiquity*, and are content to rest our cause on *External Evidence* — on Copies, on Versions, on Fathers" (pp. B-99, 100 in *Unholy Hands on the Bible*, Volume I, 1990, Sovereign Grace Trust Fund).

20 3772 3757,1063 1526 1417 2228 5140 4863 1519 1689
οὐρανοῖς. οὐ γάρ εἰσι δύο ἢ τρεῖς συνηγμένοι εἰς τὸ ἐμὸν
heavens. where For are two or three gathered together in My
3686 1563/1519/1722/3319 846
ὄνομα, ἐκεῖ εἰμι ἐν μέσω αὐτῶν.
name. there I am in midst of them.

KJV: .... For where two or three are gathered together in my name, there am I in the midst of them.

MKJV: ..... For where two or three are gathered together in My name, there I am in their midst.

ERV: .... ⊠ ⊠ [This is true, because if] two or three people are ⊠ together ⊠ ⊠ ⊠ [believing in me], I am there ⊠ ⊠ ⊠ [with them].

NIV: .... For where two or three [come] together in my name, there am I ⊠ ⊠ ⊠ [with them].

ANALYSIS: The other new versions also have these words which testify to the omnipresence of Christ while on earth. When Jesus saw His disciples toiling away, rowing in the midst of a tumultuous sea, was He not there with them in spirit? (See John 6:21) Obviously, only God could be present everywhere in the world where two or three of His worshipers gathered together. And Jesus says here plainly that He is the One who will be there; therefore Jesus must be God, co-equal with the Father, one in essence with the Father and the Spirit.

Mt 28:20

20 5207 40 4151 1321 846
τοῦ Υἱοῦ καὶ τοῦ Ἁγίου Πνεύματος· διδάσκοντες αὐτοὺς
of the Son and of the Holy Spirit, teaching them
5083 3956 3745 1781 5213 2400 1473 3326
τηρεῖν πάντα ὅσα ἐνετειλάμην ὑμῖν· καὶ ἰδού, ἐγὼ μεθ'
to observe all things whatever I commanded you; and,behold, I with
5216 1510 3956 2250 2193 4930 165
ὑμῶν εἰμι πάσας τὰς ἡμέρας ἕως τῆς συντελείας τοῦ αἰῶνος.
you am all the days until the completion of the age.

KJV: .... Teaching them to observe all things whatsoever I have commanded you: and, lo, I am with you alway, even unto the end of the world. Amen.

MKJV: ...... teaching them to observe all things, whatever I commanded you. And, behold, I am with you all the days until the end of the world.

ERV: .... Teach [those people] to obey everything [that] I have told you. [You can be sure that] I [will be] with you always. [I will continue with you] until the end of the world.

NIV: .... [and] teaching them to [obey] everything ⊠ I have commanded you. And [surely] ⊠ I am with you always ⊠ [to] the [very] end of the age.

NRSV: ..... [and] teaching them to [obey] everything that I have commanded you. And ⊠ [remember] I am with you always, to the end of the age.

ANALYSIS: Not only does Jesus say that He will be always with His elect people, but that He will "dwell in our hearts" (Eph. 3:17). Could a created being dwell in the hearts of every child of God? Certainly, it is God only who can dwell in the hearts of the saints, and Jesus as God does so.

26

THE PROMISED SEED

Genesis 3:15

15 נָחָ֑שׁ תֹּ֣אמַר תֹּאכַ֣ל כָּל־יְמֵ֣י חַיֶּֽיךָ׃ וְאֵיבָ֣ה | אָשִׁ֗ית

set will I   And   life your   the all   shall you   and   you   your

enmity   of days   eat   dust   go shall belly

בֵּינְךָ֙ וּבֵ֣ין הָֽאִשָּׁ֔ה וּבֵ֥ין זַרְעֲךָ֖ וּבֵ֣ין זַרְעָ֑הּ ה֚וּא יְשׁוּפְךָ֣ רֹ֔אשׁ

the bruise will   He   her be- and   your be- and   the be- and   be-

head you (to)   seed tween   seed tween   woman tween   you tween

16 אֶל־הָֽאִשָּׁ֣ה אָמַ֗ר הַרְבָּ֤ה אַרְבֶּה֙ וְאַתָּ֖ה תְּשׁוּפֶ֥נּוּ עָקֵֽב׃

will I   greatly   He   woman the to   the   (of) shall   you and

increase   said   heel him bruise

KJV: ....And I will put enmity between thee and the woman, and between thy seed and her seed; it shall bruise thy head, and thou shalt bruise his heel.

MKJV: .....And I will put enmity between you and the woman, and between your seed and her Seed — He will bruise your head, and you shall bruise His heel.

ERV: ....⊠ I will [make you] and the woman [enemies to each other]. ⊠ ⊠ Your [children] and her [children will be enemies]. [You will bite her child's foot], and he will crush your head.

NIV: ....And I will put enmity between you and the woman, and between your [offspring] and hers ⊠ ; he will crush your head, and you will [strike] his heel.

NASB: .....And I will put enmity between you and the woman. And between your seed and her seed; He shall bruise you [on] the head. And you shall bruise him [on] the heel.

NRSV: .....⊠ I will put enmity between you and the woman, and between your [offspring] and hers ⊠; he will strike your head, and you will strike his heel.

REB: ....⊠ I will put enmity between you and the woman, between your [brood] and hers ⊠. [They] will strike [at] your head, and you will strike [at their] heel.

NAB: ....⊠ I will put enmity between you and the woman, and between your [offspring] and hers ⊠; He will strike [at] your head, [while] you strike [at] his heel.

ANALYSIS: Only the KJV, LITV, MKJV, NKJV, NASB of the new versions translate this verse correctly. See next page.

אַבְרָהָם עַל אוֹדֹת בְּנוֹ : וַיֹּאמֶר אֱלֹהִים אֶל־אַבְרָהָם אַל־

not   ,Abraham   to   God   said And   his   account   on   ,Abraham

יֵרַע בְּעֵינֶיךָ עַל־הַנַּעַר וְעַל־אֲמָתֶךָ כֹּל אֲשֶׁר תֹּאמַר אֵלֶיךָ

you to   says   that   All   slave-   your and   the   because your   in   it Let
girl   of   boy   of   eyes   evil be

שָׂרָה שְׁמַע בְּקֹלָהּ כִּי בְיִצְחָק יִקָּרֵא לְךָ זָרַע : וְגַם אֶת־

And   .seed your   be shall   Isaac in   for   her to   listen   ,Sarah
.also   called   .voice

KJV: ....And God said unto Abraham, Let it not be grievous in thy sight because
of the lad, and because of thy bondwoman; in all that Sarah hath said
unto thee, hearken unto her voice; for in Isaac shall thy seed be called.

MKJV: ......And God said to Abraham, Let it not be grievous in your sight
because of the boy and [because of] your slave-girl. [In] all that Sarah
has said to you, listen to her voice. For in Isaac your Seed shall be
called.

LITV: ....And God said to Abraham, Let it not be evil in your eyes because of
the boy and of your slave-girl. All that Sarah says to you, listen to her
voice, for in Isaac your Seed shall be called.

NKJV: ......But God said to Abraham, Do not let it be displeasing in your sight
because of the lad, or [because of] your bondwoman. [Whatever] Sarah
has said to you, listen to her voice, for in Isaac your seed shall be called.

ERV: ....But God said to Abraham, [Don't be worried] ☒ ☒ ☒ [about] the boy.
And ☒ ☒ ☒ [don't be worried about the] slave woman. ☒ ☒ ☒
[Do the thing that] Sarah ☒ ☒ ☒ ☒ [wants]. ☒ ☒ Isaac shall [be
your only heir].

NIV: ....But God said to ☒ [him], Do not be [so] distressed [about] the boy and
☒ ☒ your maidservant. ☒ ☒ ☒ Listen to ☒ ☒ [whatever] Sarah
tells you, because [it is through] Isaac [that] your [offspring] will be
[reckoned].

NASB: ......But God said to Abraham, "Do not be distressed ☒ ☒ ☒ because of
the lad and your maid; ☒ ☒ [whatever] Sarah tells you, listen to her
☒, for [through] Isaac your [descendants] shall be [named]."

NRSV: ......But God said to Abraham, "Do not be distressed because of the boy
and [because of] your slave woman; ☒ ☒ [whatever] Sarah says to you,
☒ ☒ ☒ ☒ [do as she tells you], for [it is through] Isaac that ☒
[offspring] shall be [named for you].

REB: ....But God said to ☒ [him], Do not be [upset] ☒ ☒ ☒ [for] ☒ ☒ the
boy and your slave-girl. [Do as] ☒ ☒ Sarah says ☒ ☒ , ☒ ☒ ☒ ☒
because [it is through] Isaac['s line] that your [name] will [be
perpetuated].

NAB: ....But God said to Abraham, Do not be distressed [about] the boy or
[about] the slave woman. [Heed the demands of] ☒ ☒ Sarah ☒ ☒ ☒
, ☒ ☒ ☒ ☒ [no matter what she is asking of you]; [for it is through]
Isaac that [descendants] shall [bear your name]."

ANALYSIS: On this verse, only the KJV, MKJV, NKJV and LITV translate
the Hebrew words correctly. The rest of them destroy the promise of
the precious Seed, Christ. See below for the fulfillment of the promise:

28

Galatians 3:16

1242   3762   114 2228 1928

16 μένην διαθήκην οὐδεὶς ἀθετεῖ ἢ ἐπιδιατάσσεται. τῷ δὲ

ratified a covenant, no one sets aside or adds to (it).   And
11   4483   1860   4690   848

'Αβραὰμ ἐρρήθησαν αἱ ἐπαγγελίαι, καὶ τῷ σπέρματι αὐτοῦ.

to Abraham were said the promises,   and to the Seed of him.
3756/3004   4690   5613/1909/4183   235 56|3/1909

οὐ λέγει, Καὶ τοῖς σπέρμασιν, ὡς ἐπὶ πολλῶν, ἀλλ' ὡς ἐφ'

Not it says. And to the seeds.   as upon many.   but as of
1520   4690   4675/3739/2076   5547 5124   3004

17 ἑνός, Καὶ τῷ σπέρματί σου ,ὅς ἐστι Χριστός. τοῦτο δὲ λέγω,

One: And to the Seed of you, who is Christ.   this And I say.

KJV: ....Now to Abraham and his seed were the promises made. He saith not, And to seeds, as of many; but as of one, And to thy seed, which is Christ.

MKJV: .....And to Abraham and to his Seed the promises were spoken. It does not say, And to seeds, as of many, but as of one, "And to your Seed," which is Christ.

NKJV: .....Now to Abraham and to his Seed were the promises [made]. He does not say, "And to seeds," as of many, but as of one, "And to your Seed," who is Christ.

ERV: ....[God made] promises to Abraham and his [Descendant]. [God did] not say, "and to [your descendants]." ⊠ ⊠ [That would mean] many [people]. But ⊠ ⊠ ⊠ [God said], "and to your [Descendant]." ⊠ ⊠ ⊠ [That means only] one [person]; [that person] is Christ.

NIV: ....The promises were spoken to Abraham and to his seed. ⊠ [The Scripture] does not say "and to seeds," ⊠ ⊠ [meaning] many [people], but ⊠ ⊠ "and to your seed," [meaning] one [person], who is Christ.

NASB: .....Now the promises were spoken to Abraham and to his seed. He does not say "And to seeds," as ⊠ [referring to] many, but x x [rather to] one, "And to your seed," that is, Christ.

NRSV: .....Now the promises were made to Abraham and to his [offspring]; it does not say, "And to [offsprings]," as of many; but ⊠ ⊠ ⊠[it says], "And to your [offspring]," that is, [to one person, who] is Christ.

REB: ....Now, the promises were [pronounced] to Abraham and to his '[issue].' It does not say ⊠ ⊠ '[issues]' ⊠ ⊠ ⊠ [in the plural], but ⊠ ⊠ ⊠ ⊠ ⊠ 'your [issue]' [in the singular]; [and by 'issue' is meant] ⊠ ⊠ Christ.

NAB: ....Now the promises were [made] to Abraham and to his [descendant]. It does not say, And to [descendants], as [referring to] many, but as [referring to] one, "And to your [descendant]," who is Christ.

ANALYSIS: In the three verses above is the promise to us of the precious Seed, the Savior. But for reasons known only to them and to God, the new versionists have deliberately changed the OT prophesies in such a way that they cannot be connected with the Spirit's announcement of the fulfillment of the promise and the prophecies. By not translating the word Seed in Gen. 3:15 and 21:12 (a word which can only mean seed in the singular), and instead in this place thrusting into the Scriptures the words offspring, brood, issue or descendants, the new

29

versions erase all the relationship between Gen. 3:16 and 21:12 with Galatians 3:16. The Spirit through Paul declares the original promise was in the singular, Seed. Those using offspring, brood, issue, etc. are using words that can be, and generally are, considered to be plural when referring to children. And to deliberately put descendants (plural) is to misrepresent what God said, and destroys entirely the statement here that this was not of many, but of one Seed, in the singular. God the Spirit carefully preserved the original prophecy, writing in all three verses the emphatic singular ("Seed," not seeds), and preserving those Scriptures through the centuries so that it was still written in the singular when the apostle Paul was to refer to it, for the Spirit knew that He would announce the fulfillment of the prophecy through the apostle Paul in the first century A.D. In the face of this marvelous Divine preservation, now these bold new versions carelessly or deliberately make it impossible for their readers to recognize and rejoice over God's care for this precious prophecy and its fulfillment.

Why not say the change could be deliberate? Were not these learned men aware of the words of Gal. 3:16, and that the basic meaning in all three places was seed. Some of them have footnotes admitting that the original word was seed.

ETERNAL

John 1:1

```
      1/722  746 2258   3056          3056 2258 4314      2316
1   'Εν ἀρχῇ ἦν ὁ λόγος, καὶ ὁ λόγος ἦν πρὸς τὸν Θεόν, καὶ
    In (the) beginning was the Word, and the Word was  with   -  God, and
    2316/2258   3056    3778/2258/1722/746  4314        2316    3956
2   Θεὸς ἦν ὁ λόγος. οὗτος ἦν ἐν ἀρχῇ πρὸς τὸν Θεόν. πάντα
3   God was the Word. This One was in beginning with      God. All things
```

KJV: ....In the beginning was the Word, and the Word was with God, and the
Word was God.

MKJV: .....In the beginning was the Word, and the Word was with God, and the
Word was God.

ERV: ....[Before the world began,] ☒ the Word was [there. The Word was there]
with God. ☒ The Word was God.

NIV: ....In the beginning was the Word, and the Word was with God, and the
Word was God.

REB: ....In the beginning the Word [already] was. The Word was [in God's
presence], and [what] God [was], the Word was.

CEV: ....In the beginning was [the one who is called] the Word. The Word was
with God, and ☒ ☒ was [truly] God.

ANALYSIS: The NASB, NRSV and NAB have the same as the MKJV and
NIV. But note how the latest new versions (REB, ERV, CEV) are
willing even to distort one of the most famous and clear proofs of the
deity of Christ. There does not seem to be any fear of God before
their eyes, or love of the Scriptures as God the Spirit breathed them
out.

Hebrews 1:3

```
    3739           165      4160     3739/5607/ 541)              1391
3   οὐ καὶ τοὺς αἰῶνας ἐποίησεν, ὃς ὢν ἀπαύγασμα τῆς δόξης
    whom indeed the ages He made;  who being (the) radiance of the glory
         6481      5287        848    5342/5037     3956
    καὶ χαρακτὴρ τῆς ὑποστάσεως αὐτοῦ, φέρων τε τὰ πάντα
    and the express image of the essence  of Him,upholding and all things
         4487       1411      848  1223,  1438    2512
    τῷ ῥήματι τῆς δυνάμεως αὐτοῦ, δι' ἑαυτοῦ καθαρισμὸν
    by the word of the  power    of Him, through Himself cleansing
         4160           266      2257  2523     1722  1188
    ποιησάμενος τῶν ἁμαρτιῶν ἡμῶν, ἐκάθισεν ἐν δεξιᾷ τῆς
    having made  of the   sins   of us,  sat down on (the) right  the
        3172     1722 5308    5118       2909       1096
4   μεγαλωσύνης ἐν ὑψηλοῖς, τοσούτῳ κρείττων γενόμενος τῶν
    Majesty    on  high; by so much  better   becoming (than) the
```

KJV: ....Who being the brightness of [his] glory, and the express image of his
person, and upholding all things by the word of his power, when he
had by himself purged our sins, sat down on the right hand of the
Majesty on high;

MKJV: .....who being the shining splendor of [His] glory, and the express image
of His essence, and upholding all things by the word of His power,
having made purification of our sins, He sat down on the right of the
Majesty on high,

ERV: ....[The Son shows the] glory [of God]. [He is a perfect copy of God's
nature. The Son] holds everything together [with] his powerful

31

command. [The son] made [people] clean from [their] ⊠ sins. Then
he sat down at the right side of the Great One (*God) in heaven.*

NIV: ....[The Son is] the radiance of [God's] glory, and the exact representation
of his being, ⊠ sustaining all things by his powerful word. [After he]
had [provided] purification for ⊠ sins, he sat down at the right hand
of the Majesty [in heaven].

NASB: ......And He is the radiance of His glory and the exact representation of
His nature, and upholds all things by the word of His power. [When]
He had made purification of ⊠ sins, He sat down on the right hand
of the Majesty on high;

NRSV: ..... ⊠ ⊠ ⊠ ⊠ ⊠ ⊠ [He is the reflection of God's] glory and the ⊠
⊠ ⊠ ⊠ ⊠ [exact imprint of God's very] being, and [he] sustains all
things by his powerful word. [When he] had made purification for ⊠
sins, he sat down at the right hand of the Majesty on high,

REB: ....[He is] the radiance of [God's] glory, the [stamp of God's very] being,
and he sustains [the universe] by his word of power. [When he] had
[brought about] purification [from] ⊠ sins, he [took his seat] at the
right hand of ⊠ [God's] Majesty on high,

NAB: ....who is the refulgence of his glory, the very imprint of his being, and
[who] sustains all things by his mighty word. When he had
accomplished purification for ⊠ sins, he took his seat at the right
hand of the Majesty on high.

NOTE 1: The new versions above present the Son as a replica of God, not
co-equal with God, not one in essence with God the Father and God
the Spirit, but only a copy, a representation, an imprint, a stamp. The
word *xarakter* is defined by Thayer as "that which has actual existence
. . . real being . . . the substantial quality, nature of a person" (#5287,
Thayer's Lexicon, p. 644). Our Lord declared it: "I and My Father are
one;" (John 10:30) — "the [one] seeing Me sees Him who sent Me"
(John 12:45 LITV). It is not written 'I am a copy, a replica, an
imprint, a stamp, a representation, of My Father.' NO! It is written, "I
and My Father are one." In what way are they one? They are one in
essence, therefore Christ is said here to be "the express image of His
[the Father's] essence, . . . "

NOTE 2: When the verse is rewritten with Man-breathed words, leaving out
the distinguishing word our, Universal salvation is being taught. For
are not these new versions saying that Christ made purification of
sins without distinction, rather than for our sins? If the blood of
Christ is sufficient for the remission of all sins, and if Christ
accomplished purification for sins, then every person would be
cleansed by His blood, and therefore all would be saved. If His blood
was insufficient, and new versions say He died for sins without
distinguishing for which sins He made purification, then all men
would go to eternal punishment because no sufficient remission of
sins was attained.

The NIV's provided purification smacks of partial redemption, with Christ
providing purification, and the rest left to man. The REB's refulgence
refutes the claim that the new versions make the Bible easier to
understand. Refulgence (radiance) is not even in some dictionaries.

What greater insult could be offered to our Savior than to have His Word say that He died to make purification for sins, yet the vast majority of mankind would be thrown into hellfire? No, but it has been written "having made purification for our sins through Himself," thus specifying that He made purification for the sins of a specific group. The omission of a little three-letter word by the major new versions has robbed Christ of the travail of His soul (Isa. 53:11), because they state that He made purification for sins without specification, and because the Scriptures describe a Judgment Day with Christ sitting on the throne, dividing the sheep from goats, and casting a large body of men into hellfire.

Since it is becoming popular again for many false prophets to preach a universal salvation, it is exceedingly important that we follow those 99% of the manuscripts which say that Christ made purification for our sins, and not for the sins of every person who ever lived.

GOD THE SON WAS THE JEHOVAH WHO SAID TO MOSES: I AM THAT I AM (Exod. 3:14)

John 8:58

```
        2036  846       2424      281  281   3004 5213 4960   11
58  εἶπεν αὐτοῖς ὁ Ἰησοῦς, Ἀμὴν ἀμὴν λέγω ὑμῖν, πρὶν Ἀβραάμ
    said  to them —  Jesus,  Truly,  truly I say  to you, before Abraham
        1096   1473/1510  142/3767 3037 2443 906    1909,  846
59  γενέσθαι, ἐγώ εἰμι. ἦραν οὖν λίθους ἵνα βάλωσιν ἐπ' αὐτον·
    came
    into being.  I   AM. they took Then stones that they might cast on Him;
```

KJV: ....Jesus said unto them, Verily, verily, I say unto you, Before Abraham was, I am.

MKJV: .....Jesus said to them, Truly, truly, I say to you, Before Abraham came into being, I AM!

ERV: ....Jesus ☒ ☒ ☒ [answered], ☒ ☒ ☒ I tell you [the truth]. Before Abraham was [born], I AM.

NIV: ....I tell [you the truth], Jesus ☒ ☒ ☒ [answered]. "before Abraham was [born], I am!"

NASB:...... Jesus said to them, "Truly, truly, I say to you, before Abraham was [born], I am."

NRSV: .....Jesus said to them, Very truly, I tell you, Before Abraham was, I am.

NAB: ....Jesus said to them, "Amen, amen, I say to you, before Abraham came to be, I AM."

CEV: ....Jesus ☒ ☒ ☒ [answered] I tell you [for certain that even] before Abraham was, [I was, and] I am.

REB: ....Jesus said ☒ ☒ , "[In very truth] I tell you, before Abraham was [born] I am."

NKJV: .....Jesus said to them, "[Most assuredly] I say to you, before Abraham was, I AM."

ANALYSIS: Although nearly all of them have "I am" at the end of the verse, those who do not capitalize "I AM" fail to reveal to the reader why the Jews picked up stones to stone Christ. It was because by saying I AM, our Lord was telling them that He was God.

John 8:24

```
    1473 3756/1510/1537 _    2889    5127    2036  3767/5213/3754
24  ἐγω οὐκ εἰμι ἐκ τοῦ κόσμου τουτου. εἶπον οὖν ὑμῖν ὅτι
    I    not  am from  —  world  this.   I said therefore to you that
        599       1722    266   5216 1437/1063/3361/ 4100
    ἀποθανεῖσθε ἐν ταῖς ἁμαρτίαις ὑμῶν· ἐὰν γὰρ μὴ πιστεύσητε
    you will die  in  the   sins   of you;  if  for not  you believe
    3754/1473/1510  599      1722     266     5216   3004
25  ὅτι ἐγω εἰμι, ἀποθανεῖσθε ἐν ταῖς ἁμαρτίαις ὑμῶν. ἐλεγον
    that I  AM. you will die  in the   sins   of you. They said
```

KJV: ....I said therefore unto you, that ye shall die in your sins: for if ye believe not that I am [he], ye shall die in your sins.

MKJV: .....Therefore I say to you that you shall die in your sins, for if you do not believe that I AM, you shall die in your sins.

ERV: ....☒ I [tell you that] you would die [with] your sins if you don't believe that I AM. ☒ ☒ ☒ ☒ ☒ ☒ ☒

NIV: ....☒ I told you that you would die in your sins; if you do not believe that I am [the one I claim to be], you will die in your sins.

NASB: ......"I said therefore to you, that you shall die in your sins; for unless you believe that I am [He], you shall die in your sins."

34

NRSV:......⊠ I told you that you [would] die in your sins, for you will die in your sins unless you believe that I am [he].

NAB: ....⊠ [That is why] I told you that you will die in your sins. [For] if you do not believe that I AM, you will die in your sins.

CEV:.........⊠ [That is why] I said you will die [with] your sins [unforgiven]. If you don't [have faith in me for who] I am, you will die, [and your] sins [will not be forgiven].

REB: ....⊠ [That is why] I told you that you would die in your sins; [and] you will die in your sins unless you believe that I am [what I am].

NKJV: .....Therefore I said to you that you will die in your sins; for if you do not believe that I am [He], you will die in your sins.

ANALYSIS: Again Jesus is telling them that He is God, the I AM, the only one who can save them from their sins. Yet only 4 (LITV, MKJV, ERV, NAB) of the new versions let the reader know why He said I AM! Note how the NIV, CEV and REB completely distort this proof of Christ's deity. The NIV goes so far as to make it only a claim, ("the one I claim to be"). You can see what adding a few words will do to rob the Scriptures of their power and authenticity.

John 4:26

```
        3752    2064   1565     312        2218  3956    3004  846
26  ὅταν ἔλθῃ ἐκεῖνος, ἀναγγελεῖ ἡμῖν πάντα. λέγει αὐτῇ ὁ
    when comes  that One, He will announce to us all things. says   to her
        2424    1473/1510      2980   4671
    Ἰησοῦς, Ἐγώ εἰμι, ὁ λαλῶν σοι.
    Jesus,    I   AM,  He speaking to you.
```

KJV: ....Jesus saith unto her, I that speak unto thee am [he].

MKJV: .....Jesus said to her, I AM, He speaking to you.

The ERV has "I am [the Messiah];" the NIV has "I who speak to you am [he];" the NASB has "I who speak to you am [He];" the NRSV has "I am [he], the one [who is] speaking to you." Also the NAB has "I am [he], the [one] speaking to you," but in a footnote they say that it could be translated I AM, a designation of Jehovah in the OT. The REB has "I am [he], the [one] speaking to you;" the CEV has "I am [that one], [and] I am speaking to you [now];" the NKJV has "I who speak to you am [He]."

ANALYSIS: Here, and in Mark 13:6; 14:62, Luke 22:70; John 18:5, 6, 8, the KJV, ERV, NIV, NASB, REB, CEV, NRSV, GNB, JWV and NKJV all fail to identify Jesus as the I AM, the Jehovah that spoke to Moses at the Bush (Ex. 3:14). By claiming Himself to be the one who said to Moses I AM THAT I AM, Christ proclaims His eternal existence, the fact that He is self-existing, underived, uncreated, independent of all except the other Persons in the Godhead! In John 8:58, the MKJV, ERV, NAB, and NKJV did identify Jesus as the great I AM, but only the MKJV, LITV, and NAB (in a footnote on this verse, the Roman Catholic version, and excepting Mark 13:6) identify Jesus as the eternal I AM in every place in the NT. Since in each of the places the naked I AM appears in the Greek, and some of the versions have just those words uncapitalized in some of the places, there was no reason to add to those simple words. And since it is Jesus who is speaking, it is at least an insensitivity to fail to give Him the title I AM, which is due to Him as God the Son.

35

```
        435   235/1537/2316 1080                    3056  4561
14  ·ματος ἀνδρός, ἀλλ' ἐκ Θεοῦ ἐγεννήθησαν. καὶ ὁ λόγος σὰρξ
    will   of man,   but  of  God were born.   And the Word  flesh
    1096        4637    1722/2254      2300              1391
    ἐγένετο, καὶ ἐσκήνωσεν ἐν ἡμῖν (καὶ ἐθεασάμεθα τὴν δόξαν
    became, and  tabernacled among us,  and  we beheld   the  glory
     848   1391/5513 3439        3844   3962   4134    5485
    αὐτοῦ, δόξαν ὡς μονογενοῦς παρά πατρός), πλήρης χάριτος
    of Him, glory    as of an only-begotten from (the) Father,  full  of grace
           225          2491      3140    4012   846          2896
15  καὶ ἀληθείας.  Ἰωάννης μαρτυρεῖ περὶ αὐτοῦ, καὶ κέκραγε
    and of truth.    John    witnesses concerning Him,  and has cried out
```

KJV: .... And the Word was made flesh, and dwelt among us, (and we beheld his glory, the glory as of the only begotten of the Father,) full of grace and truth.

MKJV: ..... And the Word became flesh, and tabernacled among us. And we beheld His glory, the glory as of the only begotten of the Father, full of grace and of truth.

ERV: .... ☒ The Word [(fn-Here, it means Christ - the way God told people about himself)] became [a man] and lived among us. ☒ We saw his glory - the glory ☒ ☒ [that belongs to] the only ☒ [Son] of the Father. [The Word was] full of grace (*kindness*) *and* ☒ truth.

NIV: .... ☒ The Word became flesh and [made his dwelling] among us. ☒ We [have] seen his glory, the glory ☒ of the [One and Only, who came from] the Father, full of grace and truth.

NRSV: ..... And the Word became flesh and [lived] among us, and we have seen his glory, the glory as of a [father]'s only son], full of grace and truth.

NAB: .... And the Word became flesh and [made his dwelling] among us, and we saw his glory, the glory as of the [Father's only son], full of grace and truth.

ANALYSIS: The NIV's "One and Only, who came from" is in no way a translation of the Nestle[25] Greek which they were supposed to be translating. The most accurate translation of the Nestle[25] Greek may be found in Marshall's Interlinear, where he translates this verse as follows: "The Word became flesh and tabernacled among us, and we beheld his glory, glory as of an only begotten from a father, full of grace and truth).

The wording of the NAB and NRSV ("father's only son") is not a translation in any sense of the original word. Only the LITV, MKJV, NKJV aand NASB translate this verse correctly.

Colossians 2:9

2596   4747   2889   3756, 2596, 5547 3754/1722
9 κατὰ τὰ στοιχεῖα τοῦ κόσμου, καὶ οὐ κατὰ Χριστόν· ὅτι ἐν
according to the elements of the world, and not according to Christ; for in
846   2730 3956   4138   2320   4985
αὐτῷ κατοικεῖ πᾶν τὸ πλήρωμα τῆς θεότητος σωματικῶς,
Him dwells all the fullness of the Godhead bodily.

KJV: ....For in him dwelleth all the fulness of the Godhead bodily.

MKJV: ......For in Him dwells all the fullness of the Godhead bodily.

MARSH: Same as MKJV.

ERV: ....☒ ☒ ☒ All [of God] ☒ ☒ ☒ ☒ ☒ lives [in Christ fully (even in Christ's life on earth)].

NIV: ....For in [Christ] all the fullness of the Deity lives [in] bodily [form].

NASB: ......For in him all the fullness of Deity dwells [in] bodily [form].

NRSV: ......For in him the whole fullness of deity dwells bodily.

REB: ....For [it is] in [Christ] that the Godhead in all its fullness dwells [embodied].

GNB: ....For [the full content of the divine nature] lives in Christ [in his humanity].

ANALYSIS: The ERV and GNB do not identify Jesus as one of the three Persons in the Godhead. While the lexicons give both *deity and Godhead as the meaning of this Greek word (theothtos - 2320), keep in mind that there are many deities in this world, but only one true Godhead,* which identifies Christ as being one in essence with God the Father and God the Holy Spirit.

Hebrews 1:8

         3011   848   4442   5395   4314   5207
8 καὶ τοὺς λειτουργοὺς αὐτοῦ πυρὸς φλόγα· πρὸς δὲ τὸν υἱόν,
and the ministers of Him of fire a flame as to but the Son.
2262   4675   2316/1519   165   165   4464
'Ο θρόνος σου, ὁ Θεός, εἰς τὸν αἰῶνα τοῦ αἰῶνος· ῥάβδος
The throne of You, God, (is) to the ages of the ages, (the) rod
2118   4464   932   4675 26   1343
9 εὐθύτητος ἡ ῥάβδος τῆς βασιλείας σου. ἠγάπησας δικαιο-
of uprightness (is the) rod of the kingdom of You. You loved righteous-

KJV: ....But unto the Son [he saith], Thy throne, O God, [is] for ever and ever: a sceptre of righteousness [is] the sceptre of thy kingdom.

MKJV: ......But to the Son [He says], "Your throne, O God, [is] forever and ever. A scepter of righteousness [is] the scepter of Your kingdom."

ERV: ....But [God said this about his] son: "Your throne, O God, [will continue] forever and ever. ☒ ☒ ☒ ☒ ☒ ☒ ☒ ☒ [You will rule] your kingdom [with right judgments]."

NIV: ....But [about] the Son [he says], "Your throne, O God, [will last] forever and ever, [and] ☒ ☒ ☒ righteousness [will be] the scepter of your kingdom."

NASB: ......But [of] the Son [He says], "Thy throne, O God, [is] forever and ever. And [the righteous] scepter [is] the scepter of [His] kingdom."

NRSV:......But [of] the Son [he says,] "Your throne, O God, [is] forever and ever, and [the righteous] scepter [is] the scepter of your kingdom."

REB: ....But [of] the Son: Your throne, O God, [is] forever and ever, [and] ☒ ☒ [the] sceptre of [his] kingdom [is] the scepter of justice.

GNB: ....[About] the Son, however, [God said]: "Your throne, O God, [will last] forever and ever! [You rule over] ☒ ☒ ☒ ☒ ☒ ☒ ☒ your kingdom [with justice]."

ANALYSIS: The added words after O God — [is] — or [will last] — put quite a different meaning on the sentence. "Your throne [is] forever and ever" allows the interpretation which agrees with those Scriptures which teach that God the Son has ruled from eternity, that He is eternal. But if "Your throne [will last] forever" is written, it gives the impression that the rulership and throne will never end, but it leaves open the interpretation that it had a beginning which is not eternal, did not exist as long as God has existed.

Note that the NASB and REB follow p46, Aleph, and B by saying his kingdom, instead of your kingdom, as all the other manuscripts have it.

---

1 John 5:20b

```
     2070        2889     3650/1722      4190      2749      1492
20 ἐσμέν, καὶ ὁ κόσμος ὅλος ἐν τῷ πονηρῷ κεῖται. οἴδαμεν δὲ
    we are, and the world   whole  in      evil     lies.    we know And
   3754   5207       2316 2240           1325    2254   1271   2443
   ὅτι ὁ υἱὸς τοῦ Θεοῦ ἥκει, καὶ δέδωκεν ἡμῖν διάνοιαν ἵνα
   that the Son    of God is come, and has given to us an understanding that
    1097           228           2070/1722     228    1722
   γινώσκωμεν τὸν ἀληθινόν· καὶ ἐσμεν ἐν τῷ ἀληθινῷ, ἐν τῷ
   we might know the  true (One),  and we are in the  true (One),  in the
   5207  848      2424    5547     3778   2076    228        2316
   υἱῷ αὐτοῦ Ἰησοῦ Χριστῷ. οὗτός ἐστιν ὁ ἀληθινὸς Θεός,
   Son of Him.  Jesus   Christ.  This  is   the    true      God.
        2222   166      5038          5442   1438    575
21 καὶ ἡ ζωὴ αἰώνιος. Τεκνία, φυλάξατε ἑαυτοὺς ἀπὸ τῶν
   and the  life  everlasting. Little children, guard   yourselves  from
```

KJV: ....and we are in him that is true, [even] in his Son Jesus Christ. This is the true God, and eternal life.

MKJV: .....And we are in Him that is true, in His Son Jesus Christ. This is the true God, and the everlasting life.

REB: ....indeed we are in him who is true, [since we are] in his son Jesus Christ. He is the true God and eternal life.

CEV: ....And [because of Jesus], we ☒ ☒ ☒ ☒ [now belong to] the true God [who gives] eternal life.

ANALYSIS: While the new versions before 1985 did not tamper with this verse, note that these two newer versions alter the sense. The REB adds the words [since we are] so that it may be construed that the person said to be "Him that is true", and, "He is the true God", is God the Father. But without those words it is plain that these words apply to Jesus Christ, and it is so connected that the words "This is the true God and everlasting life" can only apply to Jesus Christ.

The **CEV** completely changes the entire verse, nine of their words not translating the Greek, and the six that they translate properly are made to give a message that the original Greek does not give. If the lovers of God and Christ, and of their words, do not hotly contend for the sacred Deposit (1 Tim. 6:12,20; 2 Tim. 1:14), future versions will have very little testimony to the Godhood of Christ.

746   2098   2424 5547 5207   2316

1 Ἀρχὴ τοῦ εὐαγγελίου Ἰησοῦ Χριστοῦ, υἱοῦ τοῦ Θεοῦ·
[The] beginning of the gospel of Jesus Christ, Son - of God,

5613   1125   1722   4396   2400 1473 649

2 Ὡς γέγραπται ἐν τοῖς προφήταις, Ἰδου, ἐγώ ἀποστέλλω
As it has been written in the prophets. Behold, I send

KJV: ....The beginning of the gospel of Jesus Christ, the Son of God;

MKJV: .....The beginning of the gospel of Jesus Christ, [the] Son of God;

The NIV, NASB, NRSV, REB, NAB, ERV, CEV all have a footnote saying, 'Some mss. omit Son of God.' Thus far the text is not disturbed, but only a disturbing footnote. However, let us keep in mind that historically yesterday's footnote becomes today's Bible text unless the true saints of God rise up and show their indignation. But as an example of how little reason there is behind these footnotes, here is the evidence:

Evidence for omitting Son of God: Codex Sinaiticus (Aleph), cursives 28, 255, Origen. Metzger also claims Codex Theta with these, "and a few other manuscripts." Since Metzger does not specify what mss. these few are, very probably they are Latin mss., a source the critics usually do not count.

Evidence for the authenticity of Son of God: All other uncials, all other cursives (over 2,000 mss. have these words), Irenaeus (170 A.D.) emphatically defended the words, citing them more than once as the proof that Jesus was God, along with Romans 1:1-4; 9:5; Gal. 4:4, 5. That was 80 years before Origen omitted the words. Burgon quotes Severianus, Porphyry (270 A.D.), and Cyril of Alexandria also positively defending the words. As for the six fathers that Tischendorf uses to defend Aleph's omission, Burgon shows that they were only quoting Origen, and often with the intention of showing that he was wrong.

Note this: If a footnote were to appear in the new versions for every place where there was an omission in Aleph, or a contrary opinion by Origen (himself a Gnostic), these new versions would be so fat they would be doubled or tripled in size. Then why a footnote here? Whenever the Godhood of Jesus Christ has been questioned by the Gnostics, Socinians, Arians, etc., and when Christ's eternal Sonship has been doubted or omitted from the Egyptian mss., there you will usually find that the testimony has been removed from the text without a footnote. OR if there is a footnote it will tend to throw doubt on Christ's deity. Will we ever see the day when the new version footnotes will say, A few mss. omit, rather than the misleading, some mss. omit?

191	2424 3754	1544	846 1854	2147

35 Ἤκουσεν ὁ Ἰησοῦς ὅτι ἐξέβαλον αὐτὸν ἔξω· καὶ εὑρὼν
heard   Jesus   that they threw   him   outside, and   finding

846	2036	846 4771	4100	1519	5207	2316	611

36 αὐτόν, εἶπεν αὐτῷ, Σὺ πιστεύεις εἰς τὸν υἱὸν τοῦ Θεοῦ : ἀπε-
him.   He said to him.   You do believe   in   the Son   —   of God?

KJV: ....Dost thou believe on the Son of God?

MKJV: .....Do you believe on the Son of God?

NIV: ...."Do you believe in the Son of Man?

NASB, NRSV, NAB, GNB: Same as NIV, saying the Son of Man, instead of the Son of God.

REB: ....Have you [faith] in the Son of Man?

ANALYSIS: What is so bad about calling Christ *the Son of Man? Did not Christ repeatedly refer to Himself by this title? Yes, but Christ never tells anyone to believe in (eis - into)* the Son of Man (which Morris admits, John, p. 494). It is very important here because once more the new versionists are depending on Egyptian mss. p66, p75, Aleph, B, D, and W, six corrupt manuscripts against 99.9% of all the evidence. The removal of God, Christ, Lord, and other references to Christ as God is simply endemic in those six mss. To deny that there is a systematic attempt to alter the Scriptures in the early centuries (so as to detract from the Godhood of Christ) is to fly in the face of an abounding array of historical references in the patristic literature. Note that the Devil and his demons never refer to Christ as *the Son of Man.* But men who believe that Christ was a created Being are quick to seize an opportunity to portray Him as Man, rather than as Godman.

See Phil. 4:13 for another case where they replaced Christ with him, leaving the verse open to a claim that the Gnostic concept of a non-Trinitarian God would be applied. See Col. 1:2 where they remove *Lord Jesus Christ* with no more evidence than Codices B and D. See Rom. 1:16 where the new versions have a gospel, but it is not *the Gospel of Christ,* according to only four Egyptian manuscripts, Aleph, A, B, and D.

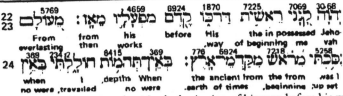

KJV: ....The LORD possessed me in the beginning of his way, before his works of old.

MKJV: .....The LORD possessed Me in the beginning of His way, from then, before His works of old.

NKJV: .....The LORD possessed me at the beginning of His way, Before His works of old.

ERV: ....[I (Wisdom) was the first thing made, long ago] in the beginning.

NIV: ....The LORD [brought] me [forth as the first] of his works, before his deeds of old.

NASB: .....The LORD possessed me [at] the beginning of His way, before His works of old.

NRSV: .....The LORD ☒ [created] me [at] the beginning of his [work], ☒ ☒ , [the first of] his [acts of long ago].

REB: ....The LORD [created] me [the first] of his [works], [long ago], before [all else that he made].

NAB: ....The LORD [begot] me, [the first born of] his [ways], [the forerunner of his prodigies of long ago].

ANALYSIS: This is the wisdom chapter which has been regarded as a testimony to the eternity of God the Son. But only the KJV, LITV, MKJV, NKJV and NASB translate it as a testimony to Him. The NIV, NRSV, and REB all make the verse read only of wisdom; or if it is still interpreted as of God the Son, they make Him a created being. So many times these modern versions accept the Gnostic idea that the Son was a being who was created first, and then was enabled to be a creator, etc. To make the Son a created being is pure heresy, as is proven by dozens of Scriptures. And that brings up the willingness of modern versionists to put plain contradictions in their versions. The true Scriptures do not have such contradictions.

41

1

רְהוּדָה בְּאַלְפֵי צָעִיר לִהְיוֹת אֶפְרָתָה בֵּית־לֶחֶם וְאַתָּה

3063	505	1961	6810	672	1035	
Judah,	the among of thousands	being	least	,Ephratha	Bethlehem	,you And

מִקֶּדֶם וּמוֹצָאֹתָיו בְּיִשְׂרָאֵל מוֹשֵׁל לִהְיוֹת יֵצֵא לִי מִמְּךָ

6924	4163	3478	4910	1961	3318	
(been have) old of from	His and forth comings	,Israel in	one ruling	be- to come forth come	shall He to Me	of out you

2

אֶחָיו וְיֶתֶר יְלֵדָה יוֹלֵדָה עֵת־עַד יִתְּנֵם לָכֵן עוֹלָם מִימֵי

251	1499	3205	3205	6256/5704	54:14	3651	5769	3117
His brothers of rest	the then given has	one the ;birth time	the birth giving (over)	the until them give	will He fore	There- .eternity	the from of days

3

בָּאוּ יְהוָה בְּעֹז וְרָעָה וְעָמַד יִשְׂרָאֵל עַל־בְּנֵי יָשׁוּבוּן

1347	3068	5797	7462	5975	3478	1121	7725
the in of majesty	,Jehovah of strength	the in (us)	pas- and ture	and He stand shall	.Israel	the of sons	shall return

KJV: ....But thou, Bethlehem Ephratah, [though] thou be little among the thousands of Judah, [yet] out of thee shall he come forth unto me [that is] to be ruler in Israel; whose goings forth [have been] from of old, from everlasting.

MKJV: ......And you, Bethlehem Ephratah, you being least among the thousands of Judah, out of you He shall come forth to Me, to become Ruler in Israel, He whose goings forth have been from of old, from the days of eternity.

ERV: ....But you, Bethlehem Ephrathah, are [the] smallest ☒ ☒ ☒ ☒ [town in Judah]. [Your family is almost too small to count]. [But] from you will come ☒ ☒ ☒ [my] "Ruler of Israel." ☒ ☒ [His beginnings come] ☒ ☒ from ancient [times], from the days of eternity.

NIV: ....But you, Bethlehem Ephrathah, [though you] are small among the [clans] of Judah, out of you ☒ will come ☒ [for] me [one who will be] ruler [over] Israel, whose [origins]* are from of old, from ancient times.

NASB: .....But [as for] you, Bethlehem Ephrathah, ☒ ☒ ☒ [Too] little [to be] among the [clans] of Judah. From you [One] will go forth [for] Me to be ruler in Israel, His goings forth are from [long ago] ☒ ☒ ☒ ☒ .

NRSV: .....But you, O Bethlehem of Ephrathah, ☒ ☒ ☒ ☒ ☒ ☒ [who are one of the little clans] of Judah, from you ☒ shall come forth [for] me [one who is] to ☒ [rule] in Israel, whose [origin]* is from of old, from [ancient] days ☒ ☒.

REB: ....But [from] you, Bethlehem [in] Ephrathah, ☒ ☒ ☒ ☒ [small as you are] among ☒ ☒ ☒ Judah's [clans], from you will come [a king for] ☒ me [over] ☒ ☒ ☒ ☒ Israel, [one] whose [origins]* are ☒ ☒ ☒ [far back in the past, in ancient [times] ☒ ☒ ☒ ☒.

NAB: ....But you, Bethlehem Ephrathah, ☒ ☒ [too] small [to be] among the [clans] of Judah. From you shall come forth [for] me ☒ ☒ ☒ ☒ [one who is] to be ruler in Israel; whose [origins]* from of old, from [ancient times].

*footnote: goings out

42

ANALYSIS: Most of this verse is quoted in Matthew 2:6, and there the new versions stick closer to the original. But in this OT passage, once again you see these new versionists denying the eternal existence of the Godman, making Him to have origins — but Jesus is God, and God has no origin.

Additionally, their translating of #505 as clans is unnecessarily putting an alien meaning on the word (which clearly means thousands). It is evident how much new versionists like to add words, and to ignore Hebrew words, as you will see by the bracketed words above, and the ⊠ ['s] denoting words not translated. What spirit is abroad which constrains men to use words that rob the Godman of His eternal existence?

Bruce Metzger, haled as the textual critic *par excellence*, wrote this about this verse: "This is the verse the Jehovah's Witnesses (along with Arians of every age) appeal to most frequently to confirm their view that Jesus Christ was a created Being" (Bruce M. Metzger, "The Jehovah Witnesses and Jesus Christ" *Theology Today*, 15:80, April, 1953). Yet Metzger headed the translation committee of the *NRSV*, which joined other new versions in presenting as Scripture the phrase "whose origin is from of old, from ancient days" — see above.

We repeat, Jesus Christ is God, and God has no origin!

Hebrews 2:11

```
         1223   3804        5048        5037/1063/ 37              37
    11  διὰ παθημάτων τελειῶσαι. ὅ τε γὰρ ἁγιάζων καὶ οἱ ἁγιαζό-
        through sufferings  to perfect.  He both For sanctifying and  the  being
              1537/1620     3956      1223/3739/ 166  3756   1870
        μενοι, ἐξ ἑνὸς πάντες· δι' ἣν αἰτίαν οὐκ ἐπαισχύνεται
        sanctified of one  all (are);  for which  cause  not  He is ashamed
            80      846    2564      3004      518           3686   4675
    12  ἀδελφοὺς αὐτοὺς καλεῖν, λέγων, 'Απαγγελῶ τὸ ὄνομά σου
        brothers   them    to call,  saying,   I will announce the name of You
```

KJV: ....For both he that sanctifieth and they who are sanctified [are] all of one: for which cause he is not ashamed to call them brethren,

MKJV: .....For both He who sanctifies and [they] who are sanctified are all of One, for which cause He is not ashamed to call them brothers,

NASB: .....For both He who sanctifies and [those] who are sanctified are all from one [Father]; for which reason He is not ashamed to call them brethren

NIV: ....⊠ Both the [one] [who makes men holy] and [those] who are [made holy] are [of the same family]. So Jesus is not ashamed to call them brothers.

NRSV: .....For ⊠ the [one] who sanctifies and [those] who are sanctified ⊠ all ⊠ ⊠ [have one Father]. For this reason [Jesus] is not ashamed to call them brothers [and sisters]

REB: ....for ⊠ he who consecrates and [those] who are consecrated are all of one [stock]. [That is why he does not shrink from] calling [men] brothers

NAB: ....⊠ ⊠ He who consecrates and those who are being consecrated all have one [origin]. Therefore, he is not ashamed to call them "brothers,"

43

GNB: ....⊠ ⊠ He [makes men pure from their sins, and both he and [those who are made pure] all [have the same Father]. [That is why] he is not ashamed to call them [his] brothers.

CEV: ....⊠ ⊠ Jesus ⊠ ⊠ and [the people he makes holy] ⊠ all [belong to the same family]. [That is why] he is not ashamed to call them his brothers [and sisters].

ANALYSIS: Thus far in Hebrews Jesus Christ is presented as God, one in essence with God the Father and God the Holy Spirit (1:3, 8, 10). This verse is certainly written of this same God the Son, for it is He who sanctifies. But note that the NAB again assigns an origin to Him. And the rest try to homogenize Him as equal to those sanctified, of the same family, of the same Father. Note also the breezy way new versionists have of making the Bible conform to the political agenda of our degenerate day, the NRSV, CEV adding [and sisters] as one of their contributions to the new age Bible. Yet the NRSV in a footnote admits that the Greek says only brothers.

Philippians 2:5-7

```
     1538      4648      235            2087      1538     5124    1083
 5  ἕκαστος σκοπεῖτε, ἀλλὰ καὶ τὰ ἑτέρων ἕκαστος. τοῦτο γὰρ
    each     looking at,  but    also other's things  each.    this    For
     5426      1722/5213/3739/1722  5547     2424/3739/1722/3444  2318
 6  φρονείσθω ἐν ὑμῖν ὃ καὶ ἐν Χριστῷ Ἰησοῦ· ὃς ἐν μορφῇ Θεοῦ
    think     among you, which also (was) in Christ Jesus, who in (the) form of God
     5225      3756   725        2233           1511/7470/2316/ 235
 7  ὑπάρχων, οὐχ ἁρπαγμὸν ἡγήσατο τὸ εἶναι ἴσα Θεῷ, ἀλλ'
    subsisting,   not    robbery    thought (it)    to be equal with God, but
    1438    2758        3444      1491    2983/722/ 3667          444
    ἑαυτὸν ἐκένωσε, μορφὴν δούλου λαβών, ἐν ὁμοιώματι ἀνθρώ-
    Himself  emptied,(the) form of a slave  taking.  in  likeness    of men
```

KJV: ....[Let this mind be in you], which was also in Christ Jesus: Who, being in the form of God, thought it not robbery to be equal with God: But made himself of no reputation, and took upon him the form of a servant, and was made in the likeness of men:

LITV: ....For think among you [that] which [was] also in Christ Jesus, who subsisting in [the] form of God, thought it not robbery to be equal with God, but emptied Himself, taking [the] form of a slave, having become in likeness of men,

MKJV: .....For [let this mind be in] you which also [was] in Christ Jesus, who, being in [the] form of God, thought [it] not robbery to be equal with God, but made Himself of no reputation, and took upon Himself [the] form of a servant, and was made in [the] likeness of men,

ERV: ....⊠ ⊠ ⊠ [Your attitude should] be ⊠ ⊠ ⊠ [the same as that of] ⊠ Christ Jesus: Who, being in ⊠ ⊠ ⊠ ⊠ ⊠ [very nature] God, did not consider ⊠ ⊠ ⊠ ⊠ [equality] with God [something] to be [grasped], but made Himself ⊠ ⊠ ⊠ [nothing], ⊠ ⊠ ⊠ ⊠ ⊠ [taking] the [very nature] of a servant, ⊠ being made in ⊠ [human] likeness ⊠ ⊠ .

NIV:: ....⊠ ⊠ ⊠ ⊠ [Your attitude should be the same as that of] Christ Jesus, who being in [very nature] ⊠ God, ⊠ ⊠ did not ⊠ ⊠ ⊠ ⊠ consider [equality] with God [something] to be [grasped], but ⊠ made himself [nothing], ⊠ the [very nature] of a servant, being made in [human] likeness.

44

NASB: ..... ☒ Have this [attitude] in yourselves which [was] also in Christ Jesus, who, [although He] existed in [the] form of God, did not regard ☒ ☒ ☒ [equality] with God [a thing to be grasped], but emptied Himself, taking [the] form of a bond-servant, and being made in [the] likeness of men

NRSV: ..... ☒ Let [the same] mind be in you that [was] in Christ Jesus, who, [though he] was in [the] form of God, did not regard ☒ ☒ ☒ [equality] with God as [something to be exploited], but emptied himself, taking ☒ ☒ the form of a slave, being [born] in [human] likeness.

REB: .... ☒ ☒ [Take to heart] among yourselves [what you find] ☒ in Christ Jesus: ☒ [He] was in [the] form of God; [yet] [he laid no claim to equality] with God, but [made himself nothing, assuming the] form of a slave. [Bearing the human] likeness,

NAB: .... ☒ ☒ Have among yourselves [the same attitude] that is [yours] ☒ ☒ in Christ Jesus, Who, [though he] was in [the] form of God, did not regard [equality] with God [something to be grasped]. Rather, he emptied himself, taking [the] form of a slave, coming in [human] likeness.

ANALYSIS: Note the many added words that all the versions feel free to insert, much misrepresenting the original God-breathed words. **Attitude** is a noun, and the word to be translated is a verb which means to **think**. It is the same idea as that expressed by the apostle Paul in 2 Cor. 10:5: "bringing into captivity every thought into the obedience of Christ." To be like Christ, we must think like Christ. And what about that demeaning translation which would have us believe that Christ made himself nothing (ERV, NIV)? The REB even goes so far as to flatly deny the import of the verse and of many other verses in which Christ claimed equality with God, by saying, 'he laid no claim to equality.' The REB contradicts itself, saying in John 10:30, "I and the Father are one." GNB has this heretical statement in verse 6: 'he did not think that by force he should try to become equal with God' — Oh to think that the American Bible Society should put out such a book and call it a Bible! And they have distributed 35 million of this God-dishonoring version, mostly to third world countries.

If nothing else, the above verses should be proof enough that the new versionists are not interested in merely translating the Greek words, but are intent on putting their own construction on them. At best they are writing commentaries; at worst they are seeking to write new Scripture according to their own minds.

47 τὸ ψυχικόν, ἔπειτα τὸ πνευματικόν. ὁ πρῶτος ἄνθρωπος ἐκ
the natural; afterward the spiritual.   The first man (was) out of
γῆς, χοϊκός· ὁ δεύτερος ἄνθρωπος, ὁ Κύριος ἐξ οὐρανοῦ.
earth, earthy; the second   Man   the   Lord out of Heaven.
48 οἷος ὁ χοϊκός, τοιοῦτοι καὶ οἱ χοϊκοί· καὶ οἷος ὁ ἐπουράνιος.
Such the earthy, such   also the earthy ones; and such the heavenly Man.
49 τοιοῦτοι καὶ οἱ ἐπουράνιοι· καὶ καθὼς ἐφορέσαμεν τὴν εἰκόνα
such   also the heavenly ones. And as   we bore   the   image

KJV: ....The first man man [is] of the earth, earthy: the second man [is] the Lord
from heaven. As [is] the earthy, such [are] they also that are earthy:
and as [is] the heavenly, such [are] they also that are heavenly.

MKJV: ......The first man [was] out of earth, earthy; the second Man [was] the
Lord from Heaven. Such the earthy man, such also the earthy ones.
And such the heavenly [Man], such also the heavenly ones.

ERV: ....The first man [was of the dust] ☒ of the earth, ☒; the second man ☒
☒ from heaven. As was the earthly man, so ☒ [are] those [who are]
of earth.

NIV: ....The first man [was of the dust of [the] earth, the second man x x from
heaven. As [was] the earthly man, so x [are] those [who are] of [the]
earth; and as [is] the man [from] heaven, so also [are] those [who are]
of heaven.

NASB: .....The first man [is] from [the] earth, earthy; the second man [is] ☒ ☒
from heaven. As [is] the earthy ☒ , so also those [who are]; and as [is]
the heavenly, so also are those who are heavenly.

NRSV: .....The first man [was] from [the] earth, [a man of dust; the second man
[is] ☒ ☒ ☒ heaven. [As was the] man [of dust, so are those who are
of the dust] and as is the man of heaven, so are] those who are of
heaven.

REB: ....The first man [is] from earth, [made of dust]; the second man [is] ☒
☒ ☒ from heaven. ☒ ☒ ☒ [The] man [made of dust] ☒ ☒ ☒ ☒
☒ [is the pattern of all who are made of dust], and ☒ the heavenly
[man is the pattern of all the] heavenly.

NAB: ....The first man [was] from [the] earth, earthy; the second man ☒ ☒
heaven. As was the earthy one, so also [are the earthy; and as [is] the
heavenly one, so also [are] the heavenly.

ANALYSIS: Note that all these new versions are leaving out those important
words, the Lord. Why? This verse became a battleground as early as
the very first century. Heretics argued that if the true reading is "The
second Man [was] the Lord from Heaven," then He could not have
taken upon Himself flesh. So they deleted the word man from their
manuscripts, and the Gnostic Marcion's text so reads: 'the second
[was] Lord from heaven.'

But this destroyed the balance which had been carefully crafted into the
sentence (the first man is balanced against the second Man; then
earthy is balanced against the Lord). So at some time in that early
century, the words the Lord were dropped in an effort to eliminate
the out of balance sentence. In the third century Origen and Cyril of

Alexandria quoted the verse both with and without **man** and **the Lord**. But in fourth century Egypt, the Gnostic codices Aleph, B, C, and D, followed in the 8th and 9th century by F-G and L (with both Aleph and D being corrected to read this way) returned to the maimed text, leaving out both **man** and **the Lord** from this verse. These with two cursives (nine manuscripts altogether) contain the maimed text. All other Greek manuscripts have the balanced text which includes both **man** and **the Lord**.

Again, our modern critics and versionists can be heard parroting this formula for casting out thousands of words from the Scriptures, 'Aleph and B are the best, most reliable mss.' Who is it that says so? THEY say so; it is an opinion based on their subjective judgment. But Aleph and B are constantly at odds with each other, seldom having the same words in a verse. Besides, they are honeycombed by blunders, impossible geographic and astronomical statements, flat contradictions within themselves, and between themselves, as well as thousands of omissions, transpositions, etc. How can such obviously doctored manuscripts be called 'best, most reliable,' etc.? And as for Aleph, A, C, F-G, in 1 Cor. 15:51 they have this contradiction: 'we shall all sleep, but we shall not all be changed' against all other mss. and evidence. And Codex D alone has: 'we shall all rise; but we shall not all be changed.'

It is far better to trust the vast body of mss. which read: "the second Man [was] the Lord from Heaven;" rather than these nine untrustworthy, error-filled, guides.

John 10:14

	4263	1473/1510	4166	2570	1097	1699
14 προβάτων.	ἐγώ εἰμι ὁ	ποιμὴν ὁ	καλός,	καὶ	γινώσκω	τὰ ἐμά,
	sheep.	I	am the Shepherd	Good,	and	I know	— Mine,
	1097		5259	1699	2531	1097	3165	3962
15 καὶ γινώσκομαι	ὑπὸ	τῶν ἐμῶν.	καθὼς	γινώσκει	με ὁ	πατήρ,
	and am known	by	— Mine.	As	knows	Me the Father.

KJV: ....I am the good shepherd, and know my [sheep], and am known of mine.

MKJV: .....I am the Good Shepherd, and I know those *(ta)* that [are] Mine, and I am known by those [who are] Mine.

NKJV: .....I am the good shepherd; and I know [My sheep], and ⊠ am known by [My own].

NIV: ....I am the good shepherd; ⊠ I know ⊠ ⊠ [my sheep] ⊠ and [my sheep know me].

NASB: .....I am the good shepherd; and I know [My own], and [My own know Me].

NRSV: .....I am the good shepherd. ⊠ I know [my own] and [my own know me].

REB: ....I am the good shepherd; ⊠ I know [my own] and [my own know me].

NAB: ....I am the good shepherd, and I know ⊠ ⊠ mine, and mine [know me].

15 καὶ γινώσκομαι ὑπὸ τῶν ἐμῶν. καθὼς γινώσκει με ὁ πατήρ,
1097 5259 1899 2531 1097 3165 3962
and am known by — Mine. As knows Me the Father,

κἀγὼ γινώσκω τὸν πατέρα· καὶ τὴν ψυχήν μου τίθημι ὑπέρ
2504 1097 3962 5690 3450 5087 5228
I also know the Father; and the soul of Me I lay down for

16 τῶν προβάτων. καὶ ἄλλα πρόβατα ἔχω, ἃ οὐκ ἔστιν ἐκ τῆς
4263 243 4263 2192/3739/3756/2076/1537
the sheep. And other sheep I have, which not are of —

KJV: ....As the Father knoweth me, even so know I the Father: and I lay down my life for the sheep.

MKJV: ......Even as (kathos) the Father knows Me, I also (kago) know the Father. And I lay down My life for the sheep.

NIV: ....Just as the Father knows me and I know the Father — and I lay down my life for the sheep.

NASB: ...... even as the Father knows Me and I know the Father; and I lay down My life for the sheep.

NRSV: ......just as the Father knows me and I know the Father. And I lay down my life for the sheep.

REB: ....as the Father knows me, and I know the Father, and I lay down my life for the sheep.

NAB: ....just as the Father knows me, and I know the Father; and I will lay down my life for the sheep.

CEV: ....Just as the Father knows me, I know the Father, and I give up my life for my sheep.

ANALYSIS: Note the distinct difference between the translation of the MKJV and all the others. In verse 14, only the KJV, MKJV, and NAB retain the important construction mine (rather than my own). Yet they miss the most important truth, which is revealed in verse 15
The major difference in these two verses is this: 996 manuscripts out of 1,000 read: "I know the ones [who are] Mine, and [I] am known by the ones [who are] Mine.

But Aleph, B, D, and L have it: 'I know My own, and My own know Me.'
What difference does it make? The Manichean heretics (c. 250 A.D.) thought it made a great deal of difference, for that is what they had in their own fabricated gospel. The heretical formulation infers that the knowledge that man has of God, and the knowledge that Christ Jesus has of God are identical, that man's knowledge and Christ's knowledge are the same. Yet the witness of 99.6% of the extant mss. is that there is an inferior knowledge that man has of God, and that there is a superior, identical knowledge that exists between the Father and the Son. The heretical change elevates man toward an equality of knowledge with God, but the manuscript evidence affirms that the original Greek elevated Christ to an equality with God, having the same knowledge between them. Once again the new versionists prefer the Egyptian mss. over every other manuscript in the world. Why? It is a personal opinion which has no basis in the evidence. In this case, there are a number of versions which have the heretical reading, especially the Old Latin and the Vulgate. Later, the Jesuit NT contains them. But normally the critics and the new versionists ignore the versions and

the Latin evidence in order to follow their cultic favorites, B and Aleph.

The evidence: The scribes of B, Aleph, D, and L have copied the Manichean heresy into their manuscripts.

Every other Greek manuscript known to us today (thousands of manuscripts and lectionaries) has the words which teach us that the knowledge that the Father has of the Son, and the knowledge that the Son has of the Father, are identical. Why wouldn't it be so, since the Son and the Father are of one essence: "I and the Father are One" (John 10:30).

But they will say that the versions, and the Latin manuscripts, and the Latin Fathers have it the same as the Manichean formulation. Yes, alas! All too often you will find the Latins in agreement with the Egyptian manuscripts, for many of the corruptions fit directly into the Roman Catholic doctrine of the equal value of Scripture and Tradition. But what of that? The critics and new versionists show nothing but contempt for the Vulgate and other Latin evidence when it opposes their subjective decisions.

Is the difference between the Egyptian manuscripts and the rest of the Greek manuscripts only a trifle? Is the co-equal deity of Christ a trifle? Then this difference is far greater than the critics would have you believe. Unless one believes that men know God in the same way that Christ knows God, then this corruption must be cast aside. Once again, it should be said that the proper name for these new versions is The Adulterated Scriptures. Or at best, The Scriptures According to Gnostic-infested Egypt in the Third and Fourth centuries.

```
        1348        2153      2198   1722   3568  165        4327
  13 δικαίως καὶ εὐσεβῶς ζήσωμεν ἐν τῷ νῦν αἰῶνι, προσδεχό-
  righteously and godly    we might live in the present age,     expecting
              3107          1680            2015              1391
      μενοι τὴν μακαρίαν ἐλπίδα καὶ ἐπιφάνειαν τῆς δόξης τοῦ
        the   blessed        hope    .and    appearance of the  glory  of the
       3173        2316    4990      2257  2424   5547    3739  1325
  14 μεγάλου Θεοῦ καὶ σωτῆρος ἡμῶν Ἰησοῦ Χριστοῦ, ὃς ἔδωκεν
      great     God and   Savior   of us,   Jesus   Christ, who gave
```

KJV: ....Looking for that blessed hope, and the glorious appearing of the great God and our Saviour Jesus Christ;

MKJV: .....looking for the blessed hope, and the glorious appearance of our great God and Saviour Jesus Christ,

ERV: .... ☒ ☒ ☒ ☒ ☒ ☒ ☒ ☒ [We should live like that while we are waiting for the coming of] ☒ ☒ ☒ ☒ ☒ our great God and Savior Jesus Christ. [He is our great hope, and he will come with glory].

NIV: ....[while we wait] ☒ for the blessed hope — ☒ the glorious appearing of our great God and Savior, Jesus Christ.

NASB: .....looking for the blessed hope and the appearing of the glory of our great God and Savior, Christ Jesus.

REB: ....looking [forward to] the happy [fulfillment of our] hope ☒ ☒ ☒ [when the splendor] of our great God and Saviour Christ Jesus [will] appear.

NRSV: .....[while we wait] ☒ for the blessed hope and the manifestation of the glory of our great God and Savior.☒ ☒

NAB: ....[as we await] ☒ the blessed hope, the appearance of the great God and our savior Jesus Christ.

ANALYSIS: All but the NAB testify to Christ Jesus as being "our great God and Savior." The NAB violates the Greek they were to translate by changing the position of the word our, making great to magnify God, rather than magnifying our Savior. Furthermore, the NAB leaves out the important words the glory of, so that the two changes serve to detract both from the glory of our Savior, and from His eternal Godhood.

The NRSV omits Christ Jesus from this verse.

Note that the NIV, NASB change from a noun (appearance) to a verb (appearing). The willingness to ignore the Divine grammar is a sign that the translator intends to rework the Scriptures into conformity to his own way of expressing things. Sometimes this does not seem to change the sense, but a change in grammar will certainly make a change in the meaning. This is especially true when a verb and noun are interchanged, as here. But myriads of such changes may be found in the new versions, mixing adjectives, adverbs, pronouns, singulars, plurals, tenses, etc. contrary to what was written as men were borne along by the Holy Spirit of God. Whose Word is this, man's word, or God's Word?

```
      3548            2999              1860      3739      3962
5  νομοθεσία και η λατρεία και αι επαγγελίαι, ων οι πατέρες,
   law-giving, and the service and the promises; of whom the fathers,
   1537/3739  5547        2596    4561   3739/1909/3956    2316
και εξ ων ο Χριστός το κατά σάρκα, ο ων επι πάντων, Θεος
and from whom the Christ according to flesh. He being over  all,     God
   2128        1519       165      281   3756/3634   3754  1601
6  ευλογητός εις τους αιώνας. αμήν. ουχ οιον δε οτι εκπιπτωκεν
   blessed      to   the   ages.  Amen.  Not, however, that has failed
```

KJV: ....Whose [are] the fathers, and of whom as concerning the flesh Christ
[came], who is over all, God blessed for ever. Amen.

MKJV: .....whose [are] the fathers, and of whom [is] the Christ according to flesh,
He being God over all, blessed forever. Amen.

ERV: .... ☒ ☒ ☒ [those people are the descendants of our great] fathers
(ancestors). ☒ ☒ ☒ ☒ ☒ [And they are the earthly family of] Christ
☒ ☒ ☒. ☒ ☒ [Christ is] God over all [things]. Praise [him] forever!
Amen.

NIV: ....☒ [theirs] are the patriarchs, and ☒ ☒ ☒ ☒ [from them is traced the
human ancestry of] Christ, ☒ ☒ [who] is God over all, forever praised!
Amen.

NASB: .....whose [are] the fathers, and from whom [is] the Christ according to
[the] flesh, [who is] ☒ ☒ ☒ over all, God blessed forever. Amen.

NRSV: .....[to them belong] the patriarchs, and [from them], according to flesh,
[comes] the Messiah, ☒ [who is] ☒ ☒ ☒ over all, God blessed
forever. Amen.

REB: ....☒ ☒ The patriarchs [are theirs], and [from them by natural descent
came] the Messiah. ☒ ☒ [May] God, [supreme] above all, be blessed
for ever! Amen.

NAB: ......[theirs] ☒ the patriarchs, and [from them], according to the flesh, [is]
the Messiah, God [who is] over all be blessed forever. Amen.

The NIV has a footnote : Or, "Christ, [who is] over all, God be forever
praised").

ANALYSIS: The NIV footnote is a gloss preferred by those who do not believe
that Christ is co-equal with God in essence and attributes. When the RV
inserted it, Burgon quoted 60 patristic fathers as using this verse to
prove the Godhood of Christ. And the Unitarians have stated that the
only two verses that needed to be changed to destroy the doctrine of the
Trinity are Romans 9:5 and 1 Tim. 3:16. The NIV undermines that
doctrine with this footnote. And they, with the other new versionists,
change 1 Tim. 3:16 in a way that completely takes away any semblance
of a witness to Christ as the second Person in the Trinity. The REB also
puts their own construction on Romans 9:5 by adding and subtracting
words, leaving no witness at this place to the Godhood of Christ in
their version.

On the subject of demeaning footnotes, the REB has this note at Luke 3:22:
"some witnesses read, You are My Son, this day I have begotten you."

That reading, if followed to its obvious conclusion, would clearly make the
Scriptures to say that Christ was a creature. And surprisingly, there is
more evidence for this heretical reading than for many that have been
accepted and inserted into the new versions' text of the NT. For it has
Codex D, the oldest Latin copies (a, gb, c, ff, l), and is quoted by Justin
Martyr and Clement Alex. in the second century, by Lactantius, Hilary,

and Juvenous in the fourth century, etc. Burgon says that it was probably an Ebionite heresy of the second century, plainly intended to teach that Jesus is a created Being (*Unholy Hands*, Vol. I, p. D-31). Yet, with far less evidence, the other new versions insert footnotes which detract from the glory of Christ as God.

---

1 Timothy 3:16

226   3672   3173 2076   2150
16 ἀληθείας. καὶ ὁμολογουμένως μέγα ἐστὶ τὸ τῆς εὐσεβείας
truth.   And   confessedly,   great is   the   of godliness
3466   2316   5319   1722 4561   1344   1722 4151
μυστήριον· Θεὸς ἐφανερώθη ἐν σαρκί, ἐδικαιώθη ἐν πνεύματι,
mystery,   God was manifested in flesh, was justified in   spirit,
3700   32   2784   1722 1484   4100/1722/ 2889
ὤφθη ἀγγέλοις, ἐκηρύχθη ἐν ἔθνεσιν, ἐπιστεύθη ἐν κόσμῳ,
was seen by angels, was proclaimed among nations, was believed in(the)world,
363   1722 1391
ἀνελήφθη ἐν δόξῃ.
was taken up in glory.

KJV: ....And without controversy great is the mystery of godliness: God was manifest in the flesh, justified in the Spirit, seen of angels, preached unto the Gentiles, believed on in the world, received up into glory.

LITV: ....And confessedly great is the mystery of godliness: God having been manifested in flesh, was justified in spirit, was seen by angels, was proclaimed among nations, was believed in [the] world, was taken up in glory.

MKJV: .....And without controversy great is the mystery of godliness: God was manifest in the flesh, justified in [the] Spirit, seen by angels, preached to the nations, believed on in [the] world, [and] received up into glory.

ERV: ....☒ ☒ ☒ ☒ ☒ ☒ ☒ [He (*Christ*) *was shown to us in a human body*] ☒ ☒ ☒ ☒ ☒ ☒ ☒]; [the Spirit proved that he was right]; [he was] seen by angels. [The Good News about him] was preached [to] the nations (*non-Jews*); [people in the world] believed in [him]; [he] was taken up to heaven in glory.

NIV: ....☒ ☒ [Beyond all question], the mystery of godliness is great: [He appeared in a body] was [vindicated] by the Spirit, was seen by angels, was preached among [the] nations, was believed on in [the] world, was taken up in glory.

NASB: .....And ☒ [by common confession] great is the mystery of godliness: [He who] was revealed in [the] flesh, was vindicated in [the] Spirit, beheld by angels, proclaimed among [the] nations, believed on in [the] world, taken up into glory.

NRSV: .....☒ ☒ ☒ ☒[Without any doubt], the mystery [of our religion] is great: [He] was revealed in flesh, vindicated in spirit, seen by angels, proclaimed among Gentiles, believed in [throughout the] world, taken up in glory.

REB: ....And ☒ great [beyond all question] is the mystery [of our religion]: [He] was manifested in flesh, vindicated in spirit, seen by angels, [he was] proclaimed among [the] nations, believed in [throughout the] world, raised in [heavenly] glory.

NAB: ....Undeniably great is the mystery of ☒ [devotion]: [Who] was manifested in [the] flesh, vindicated in spirit, seen by angels, proclaimed [to the] Gentiles, believed in [throughout the] world, taken up in glory.

GNB: ....☒ ☒ [No one can deny how] great is the ☒ ☒ ☒ [secret of our religion]. [He] ☒ appeared in ☒ [human form], was ☒ [shown to be

52

right by the] ⊠ Spirit, [and] was seen by angels. [He] was preached among [the] nations, was believed ⊠ in [the] world, [and] was taken up ⊠ ⊠ [to heaven].

JWV: ....[Indeed, the sacred secret of this godly devotion] ⊠ is admittedly great: ⊠ [He] was made manifest in flesh, was declared righteous in spirit, ⊠ ⊠ ⊠ [appeared to] angels, was ⊠ preached [about] among nations, was believed upon in [the] world, was received up in glory.

ANALYSIS: The conspirational, cultic nature of modern day critics and new versionists can be clearly seen by the common deception they display in this verse. Here is the evidence; let the reader be the judge:

For He, NO evidence whatsoever, NONE!

For who, of the uncials, ONLY Aleph, 33, 442, 2147, three lectionaries, one version (Gothic), *and not one single patristic father!* NU claims that Codex C has who, but Burgon answers: "That Aleph reads *os* is admitted. Not so Codex C, which the excessive use of chemicals has rendered no longer decipherable in this place. Tischendorf (of course) insists that the original reading was *os*. Wetstein and Griesbach (as we should expect) avow the same opinion. Woide, Mill, Weber and Parquoi being just as confident that the original reading instead was *Theos*. As in the case of Codex A, it is too late by 100 years to re-open this question. It is observable that the witnesses yield contraictory evidence" (see *Unholy Hands on the Bible*, Vol. I, pages E-7. Burgon went on to say that Wetstein was doubtful whether the cross stroke through the o was present in Codex C in 1716. Woide, on the contrary, was convinced that *Theos* had been written by the first hand, saying 'for though there *exists no vestige* of the delicate stroke which out of O makes *Theos*, the stroke written above the letters is by the first hand.... This would testify for *Theos*. "Tischendorf, so late as 1843, expressed his astonishment that the stroke in question had hitherto escaped the eyes of everyone, having been repeatedly seen by himself" (*ibid.* p. E-7). Burgon concludes, "From a re- view of all this it is clear that the utmost which can be pre- tended is that some degree of uncertainty attaches to the testimony of Codex C. Yet why such a plea should be either set up or allowed, I really do not see — except in- deed by men who have made up their minds beforehand that *os* shall be the reading of 1 Tim. 3:16 ... That Codex C is an indubitable witness for *os* I venture to think that no fair person will ever any more pretend" (*ibid.* p. E-8).

Codex C is a palimpset, that is a manuscript which had been chemically bleached and then written over. This much space given to a very doubtful claim, yet dogmatically asserted, by modern critics seemed necessary that any fairminded person might see that we have people who ignore the evidence, confidently make false claims, and seek to establish God's Word by subjective opinion, rather than by the external evidence.

For which, D, 5 ancient versions, and 2 late fathers.

For God, A, C^{vid}, F/G^{vid}, K, L, P, over three hundred cursives and lectionaries (including four cursives that read *o theos* and one lectionary that reads *theou* (from *The Identity of the New Testament Text*, Wilbur Pickering, p. 230) (for Burgon completely proved that A read

God (*theos*) by showing that credible witnesses had seen it with their own eyes, 3 versions, and 20 Greek fathers, going back to Ignatius in the first century.

What about this 'hymn or poem' which the modern versions deceptively insert into the Scriptures? It is pure speculation, a mythic ploy used to buttress their opinion! No such hymn can be produced, nor any evidential proof that it ever existed except in the minds of critics and new versionists who have an axe to grind. Here is the footnote from the NAB: "This passage apparently includes part of a liturgical hymn used among the Christian communities in and around Ephesus. It consists of three couplets in typical Hebrew balance; flesh-spirit (contrast), seen-proclaimed (complimentary), world-glory (contrast) (NAB, p. 316) [emphasis ours]. Again, let them produce this so-called liturgical hymn. And what if they did? Would that prove that the Holy Spirit breathed out such a hymn? Or that the apostle wrote **who**, not *God*, as he was borne along by the Holy Spirit? Let us not be deceived by such starry-eyed figments of the minds of men.

The removal of God from this verse is a bald denial of the eternal Godhood of Jesus Christ. See Burgon's reply to Bishop Ellicott, in which he demolished completely all the supposed evidence of the Bishop to the extent that Ellicott dared not reply. Nor has anyone else challenged Burgon's evidence (*Unholy Hands on the Bible*, Volume I, pp. E-1 to E-30).

Jude 4

```
      4102    3921      1063/5100   444              3819    4270
  4  πίστει. παρεισέδυσαν γάρ τινες ἄνθρωποι, οἱ πάλαι προγε-
   faith,    crept in      For certain   men,    those of old having
          1519/5124    2917     765                  2316  been 2257
   γραμμένοι εἰς τοῦτο τό κρίμα, ἀσεβεῖς, τήν τοῦ Θεοῦ ἡμῶν
   previously  into this     judgment.   ungodly  the of the God  of us
  -5485 .written   3346     1519  766              ones.  3441  1203
   χάριν μετατιθέντες εἰς ἀσέλγειαν, καὶ τὸν μόνον δεσπότην
   grace,   perverting   for unbridled lust, and the  only     Master
   2316        2962    2257   2424      5547      720
   Θεόν, καὶ Κύριον ἡμῶν Ἰησοῦν Χριστόν ἀρνούμενοι.
   God, and  Lord    of us.  Jesus  Christ   denying.
```

KJV: .... For there are certain men crept in unawares, who were before of old ordained to this condemnation, ungodly men, turning the grace of our God into lasciviousness, and denying the only Lord God, and our Lord Jesus Christ.

MKJV: ..... For certain men crept in secretly, those having been of old previously written into this condemnation, ungodly [ones] perverting the grace of our God into unbridled lust, and denying the only Master, God, even our Lord Jesus Christ.

NIV: .... For certain men [whose] condemnation [was] written about long ago have secretly slipped in [among you]. [They are] godless [men], who change the grace of our God into ☒ [a license for immorality] and deny ☒ Jesus Christ our ☒ only [Sovereign and] Lord.

NASB: ..... For certain ☒ [persons] have crept in unnoticed, those who were ☒ ☒ long beforehand marked out ☒ [for] this condemnation, ungodly [persons [who] turn the grace of our God [into] licentiousness and deny our only Master ☒ and Lord, Jesus Christ.

NRSV: ..... For certain ☒ [intruders] have stolen in [among you], ☒ [people] who long ago were ☒ [designated for] ☒ this condemnation [as] ungodly, who pervert the grace of our God into licentiousness and deny our only Master ☒ and ☒ Lord, Jesus Christ.

REB: .... ☒ Certain ☒ [individuals] have [wormed their way in, the very people] whom scripture] long ago ☒ [marked down for the] ☒ ☒ [sentence they are now incurring]. [They are enemies of religion; they] ☒ pervert the free favour of our God into licentiousness, ☒ [disowning] Jesus Christ, our only Master ☒ and Lord.

NAB: .... For [there have been] certain ☒ [intruders], who long ago were ☒ designated for this condemnation, godless [persons], who pervert the grace of our God [into] licentiousness and who deny our only Master ☒ and Lord, Jesus Christ

CEV: .... ☒ ☒ Some godless people have sneaked in [among us and] ☒ ☒ ☒ ☒ [are saying, "God is kind, and so it is all right to be immoral"], ☒ ☒ ☒ ☒ [They even] deny [that we must obey] Jesus Christ [as] our only Master ☒ and Lord. [But] long ago [the Scriptures warned that these] godless [people were doomed].

ANALYSIS: Thomas Manton, the great Puritan expositor, commented on this verse: "I now come to the last part of their description, *and denying the only Lord God, and our Lord Jesus Christ*. Observe their sin, denying. The object, The Lord Jesus Christ, who is here described three ways: (1) By his absolute rule and supremacy, *despothn monon*, the only Lord, (2) By his essence, *Theon, God*. (3) By his headship over the church, *kurion hmon, our Lord Jesus Christ*" (*Jude*, p. 155, Sovereign Grace Book Club, 1958). Manton proceeds on page 161 to state the reason for objecting to the removal of the Godhood of Jesus Christ from this verse: "It would seem a strange thing that I should go about to prove the Godhead of Christ, were not blasphemy grown so common, and appearing abroad with so bold a forehead. Heretofore it was a grievous abomination to the children of God when such a thought rushed into their minds; but now some promote it as a settled opinion. It is Satan's policy to loosen a cornerstone, though he cannot wholly pull it out; he striveth all that he can to make the main articles of religion seem at least questionable" (*ibid.*, p. 161, 162). Manton goes on to cite most of the verses discussed in this book to prove that Christ is God, one in essence with God the Father and God the Spirit.

Before giving our analysis of the above corruptions inserted into this verse by the major new versions, we thought it well to show that the exegetical giants of the past agree that this verse in its original language teaches that Jesus Christ is God, Lord, and Master.

First, note that in the original (supported by virtually all the Greek mss. known to us today) God appears twice not just once, yet every one of the new versions except the KJV, LITV, MKJV, NKJV strip away God from its rightful place after Master, or Lord (*despothn* - which may be translated either way; the KJV has Lord 5 times and master 5 times). The Gnostics, when given the opportunity, would remove God when it was in the vicinity of Christ in the text. The adoration of a few Egyptian mss. by the critics, the Nestle[26]/United Bible Society[3] scrapped-together Greek, and, alas! by the new versionists, causes them to follow those adulterated manuscripts whenever their Gnostic-like corruptions delete proofs of the Godhood of Jesus. Keep in mind that they do NOT follow those favored manuscripts when they agree with the majority of manuscripts against their own cultic opinions. For examples:

In Matt. 8:18, the NASB takes B alone against all other mss. In Matt. 9:34, the REB takes D against the other mss. In Matt. 19:29, the NASB, NIV, NAB take B against all the rest. In Matt. 21:44, the NRSV, GNB omit the entire verse on the basis of D alone, in spite of the fact that more than 3,000 omissions occur in that mss. In Matt. 23:4, the REB is willing to cast out four God-breathed words on the basis of L, a ninth century mss. In Matt. 23:19, they go against B. In Matt. 27:17, the REB, NRSV, GNB, and NAB have Jesus Barabbas (bracketed), with only Theta, another late mss. as their 'authority.'

In Mark 1:41, the REB steals away two precious words (*with pity*) due to their reliance on the omission-full Codex D alone. Again in Mark 6:23, the NRSV, GNB, and NAB rely on D to add 5 words, and this from a manuscript that is notorious for adding man-breathed words to the Scriptures. In Mark 7:28, the REB, NRSV, GNB, AND NAB take p45, D, and W against B and Aleph. Mark 16:9-20 are called doubtful on the basis of B (which has an empty space where these verses belong, the only empty space in the mss.) and Aleph (where the words after Mark 16:8 become larger, with much more space between letters, the only place in the mss. where this kind of subterfuge is attempted). For dozens of other examples, see *Unholy Hands on the Bible*, Volume II, pp. 19-118 (Lafayette, IN: Sovereign Grace Trust Fund, 1992)

The NIV translation committee opened a pandora's box when they decided to allow the rewriting of the Scriptures. Such a decision necessarily involves a judgment that though the Scriptures were *God-breathed* (their own translation in 2 Tim. 3:16), the choice of language and grammatical construction chosen by God the Holy Spirit to make up the Scriptures was not sufficient for the twentieth century. No, they must improve on the wisdom of the Holy Spirit by adding words, and casting out words, in order to meet their own cherished goal: smooth-reading, stylish words that will go down easily. NOTE: They have added 15 of their own words in this verse (which we have enclosed in brackets, since they never identify words they have added). They have mistranslated *aselgeian (#766)* as *immorality*, a word too weak to describe the *unbridled lusts* Jude is describing. Last, but certainly not least, they have expelled the second appearance of God in this verse, and moved the words around in such a manner that leaves the Lord Jesus Christ as Lord and Master, but NOT God. Was not that Egyptian keen, the one who removed God just before Jesus Christ? Would he not have exulted if he had known that 15 or more centuries later his version of this verse would still be in vogue among those who believe that the Scriptures are written in wax, subject to change in any generation?

The **NASB** removes God after Master, thus destroying the witness of this verse to the Godhood of Christ. By translating *metatithentes (#3346)* as *turn*, they fail to convey the seriousness of the action of the ungodly ones. In this context the word clearly means *to pervert*, as several versions recognize.

The **NRSV** translation is closer to the original. Sadly, they defeat the purpose of the verse, which is to contrast the perversion of the ungodly with those who believe that Jesus Christ is not only Lord and Master, but more importantly, that He is God. By following 1/2 of 1% of the evidence, once again the NRSV has stolen away the one key word which identifies Christ as God, one in essence with the other two Persons in the Trinity.

The **REB**, at times far more reckless in altering God's Word than the NIV, have added 22 words to this verse. None of these are needed, but rather they are used to distort the meaning of the verse. The attempt to paraphrase is often a failure simply because God's thoughts are higher than our thoughts. Worse, yet, we cannot see the whole plan of salvation as God does. It is inevitable, then, that any attempt to rewrite Scripture by adding to and subtracting from its original words will only distort the message God intended. As it stands, the REB rendition is a poor representation of what God wrote. But, again, their failure to follow the vast body of evidence has caused them to eject *God* from the vicinity of Jesus Christ, leaving the verse without a testimony to the Godhood of Christ.

The **NAB** Roman Catholic translators upon occasion are closer to the original than the other five major new versions. But in chaining themselves to the politically correct, but factually wrong, view of the textual critics, lovers of the Egyptian manuscripts, they have fallen short again. Their version of the verse also leaves Christ without His Godhood.

The **CEV** displays the very essence of Eugene Nida's theory that the Scriptures can be broken up into 'kernels,' the phrases and words moved around and placed in different connections, and yet remain God's Word. What results is what might be called The Scriptures According to Man. No less than 33 of the 49 words the CEV has reported are without backing in the Greek they were to translate. But they DO follow the NU text when they leave out *God* at the end of the verse, destroying Jude's obvious intention to testify that Christ Jesus is God.

On the translation of *kai* as *even* after *Master (Lord)*, so the word can be, and often is, translated (as in Jude 23). So we read, "and denying the only Master, God, even our Lord Jesus Christ. But also with *kai* translated as *and*, the verse still testifies to the essential Godhood of Jesus Christ.

```
      3992    846    281   281    3004  5213 3754           3056 3450
24  ψαντα αὐτόν.   ἀμὴν ἀμὴν λέγω ὑμῖν ὅτι ὁ τὸν λόγον μου
    having sent Him.   Truly,  truly,  I say  to you, The (one) the word  of Me
      191    4100          3992   3165 2192 2222  166
    ἀκούων, καὶ πιστεύων τῷ πέμψαντί με, ἔχει ζωὴν αἰώνιον· καὶ
    hearing,  and  believing the (One) having sent Me, has  life  everlasting and
    1519 2920 3756 2064     235    3327   1537    2288    1519
    εἰς κρίσιν οὐκ ἔρχεται, ἀλλὰ μεταβέβηκεν ἐκ τοῦ θανάτου εἰς τὴν
    into judgment not comes,  but  has passed  out of       death  into
      2222   281   281    3004  5213 3754 2064 5610   3568  2076
25  ζωήν. ἀμὴν ἀμὴν λέγω ὑμῖν ὅτι ἔρχεται ὥρα καὶ νῦν ἐστιν,
    life.  Truly,  truly, I say to you,      comes An hour. and now  is
```

KJV: ....Verily, verily, I say unto you, He that heareth my word, and believeth
on him that sent me, hath everlasting life, and shall not come into
condemnation; but is passed from death unto life.

MKJV: .....Truly, truly, I say to you, he who hears My word and believes [on]
Him who sent Me has everlasting life and shall not come into
condemnation, but has passed from death to life.

ERV: ....☒ ☒ ☒ ☒ ☒ [I tell] you [the truth.] ☒ ☒ [If a person] hears ☒ ☒
☒[what I say] and believes [in] the [One] who sent me, [that person]
has life forever. ☒ ☒ ☒ ☒ ☒ ☒ [That person will not be judged
guilty]. ☒ [He] has ☒ ☒ ☒ [already left death and has entered] into
life.

NIV: ....☒ ☒ ☒ ☒ ☒ ☒ [I tell] you [the truth], whoever hears my word and
believes him who sent me has eternal life and will not ☒ ☒ ☒ [be
condemned; ☒ [he] has crossed over from death to life.

NASB, NRSV, NAB virtually the same as MKJV

REB: ....[In very truth] ☒ I tell you whoever ☒ ☒ ☒ [heeds what I say] and
☒ [puts his trust [in] him who sent me has eternal life; ☒ [he does]
not come to judgement, but has [already] passed from death to life.

ANALYSIS: The versions above ignore grammatical construction, and do not
have any intention of exact correspondence between the original
Greek words and the words that they add. For instance, *Amen, Amen*
(#281) is an asseverative particle which can be translated Truly, Truly.
But truth, being a noun, cannot be a translation of Amen.
Condemnation, however, is a noun, yet the NIV translates it with a
verb, condemned. Those who argue for the right to rewrite Scripture
boldly say that the Holy Spirit's Greek is not appropriate for today,
and therefore the grammar can be ignored. Is this not arguing that
God the Spirit did not have the omniscience to know what would be
appropriate language in the twentieth century? And who are these
men who claim that they have the wisdom and knowledge necessary
to write new Scripture?

John 5:25

```
   2222   281   281   3004  5213 3754  2064 5610    3568   2076
25 ζωήν. ἀμὴν ἀμὴν λέγω ὑμῖν ὅτι ἔρχεται ὥρα καὶ νῦν ἐστιν,
   life.  Truly,  truly, I say to you,   comes An hour, and now  is,
   3753   5498    191              5456      5207        2316
   ὅτε οἱ νεκροὶ ἀκούσονται τῆς φωνῆς τοῦ υἱοῦ τοῦ Θεοῦ,
   when the   dead  will hear from the  voice  of the  Son  —   of God,
            191           2198         5618 1063   3962  2192 2222
26 καὶ οἱ ἀκούσαντες ζήσονται. ὥσπερ γὰρ ὁ πατὴρ ἔχει ζωὴν
   and those hearing        will live.  even as  For  the  Father  has  life
```

KJV: ....Verily, verily, I say unto you, The hour is coming, and now is, when the dead shall hear the voice of the Son of God: and they that hear shall live.

MKJV: .....Truly, truly, I say to you, the hour is coming and now is, when the dead shall hear the voice of the Son of God, and they who hear shall live.

ERV: .... ☒ ☒ ☒ ☒ ☒ ☒ I tell you [the truth:] [An important time] is coming. ☒ [That time] is already [here]. ☒ ☒ [People that are] dead [in sin] will hear the voice of the Son of God. And [the people] that [accept the things they hear from the Son] will have life [forever]

NIV: .... ☒ ☒ ☒ ☒ ☒ ☒ ☒ ☒ [I tell] you [the truth, a] time is coming, and [has] now [come], when the dead will hear the voice of the Son of God, and those who hear will live.

NASB, NRSV, NAB virtually the same as MKJV

REB: ....[In very truth I tell] you [the time] is coming, [indeed] it is [already] here, when the dead shall hear the voice of the Son of God, and those who hear shall [come to life].

John 5:26

```
              191       2198        5618 1063   3962  2192 2222
26 καὶ οἱ ἀκούσαντες ζήσονται. ὥσπερ γὰρ ὁ πατὴρ ἔχει ζωὴν
   and those hearing        will live.  even as  For  the  Father  has  life
   1722/ 1438  3779  1326          5207 2222  2192/1722/1438
27 ἐν ἑαυτῷ, οὕτως ἔδωκε καὶ τῷ υἱῷ ζωὴν ἔχειν ἐν ἑαυτῷ· καὶ
   in Himself.   so       He gave also to the Son  life to have in Himself. And
```

KJV: ....For as the Father hath life in himself; so hath he given to the Son to have life in himself;

MKJV: .....For as the Father has life in Himself, so He gave to the Son to have life within Himself,

ERV: .... ☒ ☒ [Life comes from] the Father (God) ☒ ☒ ☒ himself. So [the Father] has ☒ ☒ [also allowed] the Son (Jesus) to [give] life ☒ ☒.

NIV: ....For as the Father has life in himself, so has he [granted] the Son to have life in himself.

REB: ....For as the Father has life in himself, so ☒ ☒ ☒ ☒ [by his gift] the Son also has life in himself.

NAB: ....For just as the Father has life in himself, so also he gave to his Son [the possession of] life in himself.

NRSV: .....For just as the Father has life in himself, so he has [granted] the Son also to have life in himself.

ANALYSIS: There is a common misunderstanding here, as evidenced by the words the new versions have chosen to thrust into the text. When it

59

says that "the Father has given to the Son to have life within Himself," it is not a gift (as the REB has it), not a granting of something the Father had before, and in another time or place granted (as the NIV and NRSV have it) to the Son to have life in Himself. Rather, we are being given insight into the eternal counsels where the Divine wisdom conceived all that would come to pass, and the allocation of the part each One of the Godhead would have in the unfolding of the ages. To God the Son it was given to bestow everlasting life to the elect people. It was His assignment in the plan of salvation. The Holy Three had chosen an elect group from among mankind, they had loved them with an everlasting love (Jer. 31:3). Every one of these were to be sinners, dead in trespasses and sin, children of wrath, even as the rest (Eph. 2:1, 2). To God the Spirit it was given to implant that everlasting life into the elect. The ultimate goal of the Gnostics was to make the Son subordinate to the Father, a lesser god whose powers were all derived from the Father. By putting their trust in the Egyptian manuscripts, the new versionists are inserting Gnostic doctrine into their versions, whether wittingly or unwittingly.

```
        2504   1097    846          190          3427   2504   2222
  28  κἀγὼ γινώσκω αὐτά, καὶ ἀκολουθοῦσί μοι· κἀγὼ ζωὴν
      and I   know    them,   and   they follow   Me;   and I   life
        166    1325    846        -3364-   622        1519   165
      αἰώνιον δίδωμι αὐτοῖς· καὶ οὐ μὴ ἀπόλωνται εἰς τὸν αἰῶνα,
      eternal   give   to them;  and in no way shall they perish for    ever,
        3756    726    5100   846 1537      5495   3450      3962  3450
  29  καὶ οὐχ ἁρπάσει τις αὐτὰ ἐκ τῆς χειρός μου. ὁ πατήρ μου
      and  not   shall pluck anyone them out of the hand of Me. The Father of Me
```

KJV: ....And I give unto them eternal life; and they shall never perish, neither shall any [man] pluck them out of my hand.

MKJV: .....And I give to them eternal life, and they shall never perish, and not anyone shall pluck them out of My hand.

ERV: ....⊠ I give ⊠ ⊠ [my sheep] eternal life. ⊠ They will never die. And no [person can] take them out of my hand.

NIV: ....⊠ I give them eternal life, and they shall never perish; ⊠ no one [can] snatch them out of my [Father's] hand.

NASB: .....And I give eternal life to them, and they shall never perish, and no one shall snatch them out of My hand.

NRSV: .....I give them eternal life, and they will never perish. No one will snatch them out of my hand.

ANALYSIS OF THE ABOVE VERSES: Again and again it has been written that Christ gives life, everlasting life, eternal life. But One must be eternal in order to give eternal life. Therefore, a created being cannot give eternal life. Yet our new versions in one place report this Divine power to Christ, then in another place they do not report God's words in a way that affirms His Godhood. Instead, they incorporate age-old heresies within their pages, many of which make Jesus Christ out to be a created Being. In such verses they are not merely being ambiguous, nor even just ambivalent, they are clearly willing to turn a jaundiced eye on the myriads of manuscripts that testify to the co-equal Godhood of Christ, and to accept the corrupt falsifications of the early heretics which deny eternal Godhood to Christ. Christ is "the Way, the Truth, and the LIFE."

We have included some verses which testify to the Godhood of Christ, and which are relatively left in their original words, so that it may be seen that in some places the new versions DO testify to this important doctrine. But by failing to follow the majority of the manuscripts, and by turning a blind eye to the corruptions in the Egyptian manuscripts, there are more verses in the new versions which deny, or weaken, testimony to the deity of Christ. This may be seen in the many verses examined in this book.

61

OMNISCIENCE

John 2:24

24 σημεῖα ἅ ἐποίει. αὐτὸς δὲ ὁ Ἰησοῦς οὐκ ἐπίστευεν ἑαυτὸν
signs which He did, Himself But, —   Jesus   not did commit   Himself
846   1222   846   1097   3956   3754/3756/5532
25 αὐτοῖς, διὰ τὸ αὐτὸν γινώσκειν πάντας, καὶ ὅτι οὐ χρείαν
to them, because(of) Him   knowing   all,   and because no   need

KJV: ....But Jesus did not commit himself unto them, because he knew all [men],

LITV: ....But Jesus Himself did not commit Himself to them, because He knew all.

MKJV: .....But Jesus did not commit Himself to them, because He knew all [men].

ERV: ....But Jesus did not trust ☒ ☒ ☒ them. [Why?] Because [Jesus] knew [the things people were thinking].

NIV: ....But Jesus [would] not entrust himself to them, for he knew all [men].

NRSV: .....But Jesus [on his part would] not entrust himself to them, because he knew all [people].

REB: ....But Jesus [for his part would] not trust himself to them. He knew [them] all.

John 2:25

846   1223   846   1097   3956   3754/3756/5532
25 αὐτοῖς, διὰ τὸ αὐτὸν γινώσκειν πάντας, καὶ ὅτι οὐ χρείαν
to them, because(of) Him   knowing   all,   and because no   need
2192 2443 5100 3140   4012   444   846   1063
εἶχεν ἵνα τις μαρτυρήσῃ περὶ τοῦ ἀνθρώπου· αὐτὸς γὰρ
He had that any should witness concerning —   man;   He   for
1097 5101/2258/1722   444
ἐγίνωσκε τί ἦν ἐν τῷ ἀνθρώπῳ.
knew what was in   man.

KJV: ....And needed not that any should testify of man: for he knew what was in man.

LITV: ....and because He had no need that anyone should witness concerning man, for He knew what was in man.

MKJV: .....and did not need that anyone should testify of man. For He knew what was in man.

ERV: ....[Jesus] ☒ did not need ☒ any [person to tell him about people]. ☒ [Jesus] knew what was in [a person's mind].

NIV: ....☒ [He] did not need ☒ ☒ ☒ ☒ ☒ [man's testimony about] man, for he knew what was in man.

REB: ....and had no need [of evidence from others about] anyone, for he [himself could tell] what was in [people].

ANALYSIS OF VSS. 24, 25: Jesus did not put His faith in these people. That is quite different from saying He would not. He was omniscient, was all-wise, knew everything and so knew all, both things and men. There is no need to add people, men etc. at the end of vs. 24, for God did not add. He knew all!

In vs. 25, the God-breathed words are simple enough. What is the need of all those added words in the new versions? Jesus, being God, knew all. No one but God knows ALL!

In these two verses the ERV demonstrates the common presumption among today's 'translators,' that it is their calling to tell the reading public what God means, not just what God says. That is to say, they presume to fix the meaning for everyone else, using their own understanding as the sure guide to the meaning of God's words.

```
    3813    3427    3004    846       2424      4198         5207 4675
50  τὸ παιδίον μου. λέγει αὐτῷ ὁ Ἰησοῦς. Πορεύου· ὁ υἱός σου
    the child   of me.   says    to him   Jesus,   Go,      the son of you
    2198        4100        444            3956/3739/2036  846
    ᾗ. καὶ ἐπίστευσεν ὁ ἄνθρωπος τῷ λόγῳ ᾧ εἶπεν αὐτῷ
    lives. And  believed   the   man         the   word which said  to him
    2424        4198      2235       846     2597
51  Ἰησοῦς, καὶ ἐπορεύετο. ἤδη δὲ αὐτοῦ καταβαίνοντος, οἱ
    Jesus,    and   went away.  already And (as)he (was) going down   the
    1401   848       528         846         518              3004
    δοῦλοι αὐτοῦ ἀπήντησαν αὐτῷ, καὶ ἀπήγγειλαν λέγοντες
    slaves  of him    met            him, and reported,        saying,
    3754   3816 4676 2198    4441  3767/3844  848         5610/1722
52  ὅτι Ὁ παῖς σου ζῇ. ἐπύθετο οὖν παρ᾽ αὐτῶν τὴν ὥραν ἐν
    - The child of you lives. He asked then from  them     the  hour   in
    37392866        2192     2036    846  3754/5504 5610     1442
    ᾗ κομψότερον ἔσχε. καὶ εἶπον αὐτῷ ὅτι Χθὲς ὥραν ἑβδόμην
    which better     he had. And they said to him. Yesterday (at)hour seventh
    863     846       4446     1097/3767  3962  3754/1722  1565
53  ἀφῆκεν αὐτὸν ὁ πυρετός. ἔγνω οὖν ὁ πατὴρ ὅτι ἐν ἐκείνῃ τῇ
    left    him  the  fever.  Knew, then, the  father that in  that    -
    5610 1722/3739/2036 848        2424   3754    5207 4675 2198
    ὥρᾳ, ἐν ᾗ εἶπεν αὐτῷ ὁ Ἰησοῦς ὅτι Ὁ υἱός σου ζῇ· καὶ
    hour in which said  to him  -   Jesus.    - The son of you lives. And
```

KJV: ....Jesus saith unto him, Go thy way; thy son liveth. And the man believed the word that Jesus had spoken unto him, and he went his way.

MKJV: .....Jesus said to him, Go, your son lives. And the man believed the word which Jesus said to him and went away.

ERV: ....Jesus ☒ ☒ ☒ ☒ [answered], "Go, your son [will] live." ☒ The man believed ☒ ☒ ☒ ☒ [what] Jesus told him and went [home]

NIV:: .... Jesus ☒ ☒ ☒ [replied], [You may] go. Your son [will] live. The man ☒ ☒ ☒ ☒ [took] Jesus ☒ ☒ ☒ [at his word] and went away.

NASB: ......Jesus said to him, Go [your way]; your son lives. ☒ The man believed the word Jesus spoke to him, and [he started off].

NRSV: .....Jesus said to him, Go, your son [will] live. The man believed the word that Jesus spoke to him and [started on his] ☒ way.

REB: ....☒ [Return home], said Jesus ☒ ☒ ; your son [will] live. The man believed ☒ ☒ what Jesus had said and [started for home].

ANALYSIS OF VS. 50: "your son lives" is in the present indicative case. Right that moment the son was alive, and the man believed that his son was alive at that moment. To put into Jesus' mouth, "your son will live" changes the meaning altogether, for this means that the man must go and see IF what Jesus said was true. Jesus knew all, being both omniscient and omnipotent, He could and did make the son well. And the man believed that Jesus could and did do this at that moment. This is not a case of "seeing is believing," but of having faith in things not being seen (Hebrews 11:1). It is also a demonstration that the changing of the grammatical construction, such as a present for a future here, changes what God wrote.

ANALYSIS OF VSS. 52, 53: The man learns that his son was healed (or resurrected) at the very hour Jesus had said, "Your son lives." But the ERV, NIV, NRSV, REB, NAB all change lives to will live, denying the omniscience of Jesus when He declared that at that moment, "Your son lives;" not, "Your son will live." This not so subtle change in the tense takes away both the omniscience and omnipotence of Jesus, and also

denies that Jesus can create faith in a man before the man can see
whether or not what Jesus said is true.

Revelation 2:23b

```
      3173      1437/3361/  3340        1537        2041     848
23  μεγάλην, ἐὰν μὴ μετανοήσωσιν ἐκ τῶν ἔργων αὐτῶν. καὶ τὰ
        great,     unless  they may repent of  the  works    of them. And the
      5043    848      615      1722     2288              1097        3956
    τέκνα αὐτῆς ἀποκτενῶ ἐν θανάτῳ· καὶ γνώσονται πᾶσαι
    children of her    I will kill  with  death;    and    will know    all
      1577     3754/1473/1510   2045        3510                2588
    αἱ ἐκκλησίαι ὅτι ἐγώ εἰμι ὁ ἐρευνῶν νεφροὺς καὶ καρδίας·
    the  churches    that  I   am the (One) searching  kidneys and    hearts,
           1325    5213    1538     2596          2041   5216   5213
24  καὶ δώσω ὑμῖν ἑκάστῳ κατὰ τὰ ἔργα ὑμῶν. ὑμῖν δὲ
    and I will give to you    each    according to the works of you. to you But
```

KJV: ....and all the churches shall know that I am he which searcheth the reins
and hearts: and I will give unto every one of you according to your
works.

MKJV: .....And all the churches will know that I am He who searches the reins
and hearts, and I will give to every one of you according to your works.

NIV: ....Then all the churches will know that I am he who searches hearts and
minds, and I will [repay] each of you according to your deeds.

NASB: .....and all the churches will know that I am He who searches the minds
and hearts; and I will give to each one of you according to your deeds.

NRSV: .....And all the churches will know that I am the one who searches minds
and hearts, and I will give to each of you as your works [deserve].

REB: ....[This will teach] ☒ all the churches ☒☒ that I am the searcher of
[men's] hearts and minds, and that I will give to each of you [what his]
deeds [deserve].

ANALYSIS: Can anyone but the Persons of the Trinity search the inner parts
and hearts of every single person in the universe? And who but God the
Son can be said to be the Judge (Rom. 14:10, which see) who will give
to each one according to their works? Note the translation of *erga*
(*#2041*) as *deeds (NIV, NASB, REB)*. We never speak of God's deeds
when that word is employed, but of His works, the total of all His acts.
While individual acts and deeds of men will be judged, there will be a
final judgment based on their works as a whole. It is false to make this
verse say that Christ will 'give to each of you as your works [deserve]'
(as the NRSV and REB say here). Giving according to our works does
not imply that we deserve anything. *"It is God who is working in you both
to will and to work for the sake of His good pleasure" (Phil. 2:13).*

DID JESUS DENY HIS GOODNESS AND HIS GODHOOD IN MATTHEW 19:16,17?

GOODNESS

Matthew 19:16,17

```
      2400  1520  4334        2036    846    1320        18
16  Καὶ ἰδού, εἰς προσελθὼν εἴπεν αὐτῷ, Διδάσκαλε ἀγαθέ,
    And behold! One coming near  said to Him,    teacher    Good
    5101 18     4160  2443 2192 2222 166                  2036    846
17  τί ἀγαθὸν ποιήσω, ἵνα ἔχω ζωὴν αἰώνιον ; ὁ δὲ εἴπεν αὐτῷ,
    what good   shall I do   that I may have life eternal? He And said to him,
    5101 3165 3004 18        3762    18    ~1508 1520 2316  1487
    Τί με λέγεις ἀγαθόν ; οὐδεὶς ἀγαθός, εἰ μὴ εἷς, ὁ Θεός εἰ δὲ
    Why Me you call good?  No one(is)good   except One. — God. if But
    2309 1525    1619       2222   5083              1755       3004
18  θέλεις εἰσελθεῖν εἰς τὴν ζωήν, τήρησον τὸς ἐντολάς. λέγει
    you desire to enter into —   life,  keep      the commands. He says
```

KJV: ....And, behold, one came and said unto him, Good Master, what good thing shall I do, that I may have eternal life? And he said unto him, Why callest thou me good? [there is] none good but one, [that is], God: but if thou wilt enter into life, keep the commandments.

MKJV: .....And behold, one came and said to Him, Good Teacher, what good shall I do that I may have eternal life? And He said to him, Why do you call Me good? [There is] none good but one, that is, God. But if you want to enter into life, keep the commandments.

NOTE: ....[In the Greek of the vast majority of the mss., Matt. 19:16,17 has the same Greek words as Mark 10:17, 18 and Luke 18:18,19].

ERV: .... ☒ ☒ [A man] came [to Jesus] and [asked]. ☒ Teacher, what [good thing must I do to] have life forever? [Jesus answered,] Why [do you ask me about what is] good? [Only] ☒ ☒ ☒ [God is] good ☒ ☒ ☒. But if you want to [have life forever,] obey the commands.

NIV: .... ☒ ☒ , Now [a man] came up [to] Jesus, ☒ ☒ ☒ ☒ , ☒ Teacher, what good [thing] must I do [to get] ☒☒☒ eternal life? ☒ ☒ ☒ ☒ ☒ Why do you ☒☒ [ask me about what is] good? [Jesus replied,] There is [only] one [who is] good. ☒ ☒ ☒ ☒ If you want to enter ☒ life, obey the commandments.

NASB:...... And behold, one came to Him and said, ☒ Teacher, what good [thing] shall I do that I may [obtain] eternal life? And He said to him, Why ☒ ☒ ☒ ☒ [are] you [asking] Me [about what is] good. There is [only] One [who is] good; ☒☒☒ but if you wish to enter into life, keep the commandments.

NRSV: ..... ☒ ☒ Then [someone] came to him and said, ☒ Teacher, what good [deed must] I do to have eternal life? And he said to him, Why [do] you ☒☒ [ask about what is] good? [There is only] one [who is] good. ☒☒☒ If you wish to enter into life, keep the commandments.

REB: .... ☒ ☒ [A man] came up and ☒ ☒ [asked] him, ☒ Teacher, what good [must] I do to [gain] ☒☒ eternal life? ☒ ☒ ☒ ☒ ☒ ☒☒☒☒ Good? said [Jesus] ☒ ☒. Why do you ☒ ☒ ☒ [ask about that?] ☒ One [alone] ☒ is good ☒ ☒☒☒☒☒. But if you wish to enter into life, keep the commandments.

65

NAB: ....Now ☒ [someone approached] ☒ ☒ ☒ him and said ☒ ☒ , ☒ Teacher, what good [must] I do to [gain] ☒ eternal life? ☒ He ☒ ☒ ☒ [answered], Why do you ☒ ☒ [ask me about the] good? [There is only] ☒ ☒ ☒ ☒ One [who is] good ☒☒☒. If you wish to enter into life, keep the commandments.

GNB: ....☒☒☒ [Once a man] came to [Jesus] ☒ ☒ ☒ ☒ , ☒ Teacher, [he asked,] what good [thing must] I do to [receive] ☒ eternal life? Why do you ☒ ☒ ☒ [ask me concerning what is] good? [answered Jesus]. [There is] ☒ ☒ ☒ only One [who is] good ☒☒☒. Keep the commandments if you want to enter life.

ANALYSIS: The CEV and JWV have much the same as the six above. Here is a prime case of Gnostic corruptions being accepted by modern critics, adding words and omitting words with the result that Jesus is not only robbed of His goodness, but is actually made to deny His own goodness. Yet these corruptions are not carried over into Mark 10:17, 18 and Luke 18:18, 19, where the same episode is reported by those two evangelists. Clearly the modern versions contradict themselves, having Jesus deny His goodness in Matthew, but not denying it in Mark and in Luke.

Both the evidence for the true reading, and the evidence to prove that Gnostics were the Devil's instrument to sully the Lord Christ, are plentiful. The enemies of the Gospel seized upon this opportunity to deny that Jesus was God, essentially good and one in essence with God the Father and God the Spirit. "Valentinus (150 A.D.), Hercleon, Ptolemaeus, the Marcosians, the Naassenes, Marcion, and the rest of the Gnostic crew not only substituted 'One is good' for *"No one is good but one,"* but gleeful over their initial success in planting this blasphemous change, proceeded to make other changes. Marcion added the Father, thus '[One is good.] *No one is good except one, God* [the Father].' This, if left in the Scriptures, completely denies the essential goodness of God the Son.

But there is more corruption: These same enemies of the Gospel also changed Jesus' question when He asked, *Why do you call Me good?* This was changed, in the manner of the modern versions, by adding and subtracting words, making Jesus to ask 'Why do you ask Me concerning the good?' Further, not content with leaving the young man saying *Good Master,* they then stole away the word *Good,* and now have nothing left in verses 16 and 17 which testify to the goodness of Jesus Christ, but rather have Him denying His own goodness.

What then is the evidence?

1. For these corruptions: Aleph, B, D, L, and cursives 1 and 22 - six MSS. Among the versions, the Latin and Bohairic have some, but not all the adulterations, as does the Thebaic. Origen appears on both sides. Burgon shows that **even Aleph and B do not have ALL the corruptions,** and he charts how those who are counted as witnesses for the false wording are divided throughout. There is not one of the surviving Greek MSS. that has all of the corruptions that one finds in the six most popular versions today.

66

2. Against these and for the reading that stood for 18+ centuries: All the other uncials, all the other 1,800+ cursives (except Evann. 479, 604 and Evst. 5, who witness on both sides). Burgon produces 18 quotations for the Received/Majority Text reading, even Justin Martyr, the Marcosians and Naassenes, etc. from the 2nd century, nearly 200 years before Aleph and B were written, 3 from the third century, 6 from the fourth century, 5 in the fifth — witnesses from every part of Christendom. To read the entire evidence, see *Unholy Hands on the Bible*, Volume I, pp. 127-134.

How, then, can Nestle, NU, WH, the major critics, and the modern versions insert into what they call the Holy Bible **every one of the corruptions** when even their idol MSS., Aleph and B, do not have **all** of them, nor do the other uncials? Even the heretic Marcion did **not** include all the heretical words! Nor did Origen, another Gnostic who did not believe in the deity of Jesus Christ. To put it bluntly, these verses in the NIV, NASB, NRSV, REB, GNB, NAB, CEV, JWV, and others are **more corrupt**, contain **more heresy** than ANY manuscript in the world! What a place for the new versions to excel, and to be completely of one mind, in the denying of the goodness of the Lord Jesus Christ, God the Son!

So these so-called experts of the last 150 years are willing to go further than the heretics of the first centuries by including every one of these corruptions in their versions. Do the modern-day 'translators' feel guilty? Apparently not, for they are not even honest enough to insert a footnote to let the reader of their adulterated versions know that there is in existence any other evidence contrary to their words. How well do the words of Jeremiah fit them: "So says the LORD, Behold! I [am] against the prophets, who steal My words, each one from his neighbor" (MKJV) And the commentators who defend these adulterations are equally guilty (See Matthew, Leon Morris pp. 488, 89). You shall know them by their fruits (Matt. 7:16).

But this should be the best evidence of all: Mark 10:17, 18; Luke 18:18, 19 have the very same words that the critics and versionists reject here in Matthew! Yet the critics and new versionists do not question Mark's or Luke's words. Note then, that the NASB, NIV, etc. have contradictory reports of what the rich young ruler said to Jesus. Did he say the words they have in Matthew? Or did he say the words they have in Mark and Luke? Is it not strange that the Gnostics did not also change the words in Mark and Luke? Is it not clear that these modern translation committees have such a low regard of God's Word that they will deliberately put contradictory reports in their versions?

JEHOVAH

Isaiah 40:3

3 זְ בַּֽמִּדְבָּ֖ר ק֥וֹרֵא ק֣וֹל ׃תֵּֽאמַ֑תְכָל־כָּֽלָים בִּ יְהוָ֖ה מֵ֣י
    the in   him   The   .sins her all for double Jehovah's from
  ,wilderness crying of voice   hand

4 גַיְא כָּל־ לֵאלֹהֵֽינוּ׃ מְסִלָּ֖ה בָּֽעֲרָבָ֑ה יַשְּׁר֖וּ יְהוָ֑ה דֶּ֣רֶךְ פַּנּ֖וּ
  valley Every   our for   a   the in   make :Jehovah the Pre-
             God highway desert straight of way pare

KJV: ....The voice of him that crieth in the wilderness, Prepare ye the way of the LORD, make straight in the desert a highway for our God.

MKJV: .....The voice of him who cries in the wilderness, Prepare the way of the LORD (Jehovah), make straight a highway in the desert for our God.

ERV: ....[Listen! You can hear] the sound [of a man] calling loudly: Prepare [a] way for the Lord in the desert! Make the road in the desert straight for our God.

NIV:: ....[A] voice of one calling "In the desert prepare the way of the LORD; make straight in the wilderness a highway for our God."

NASB: .....[A] voice [is] calling, "Clear the way for the LORD in the wilderness; Make smooth in the desert a highway for our God."

NRSV: .....A voice cries out: In the wilderness prepare the way of the LORD, make straight in the desert a highway for our God.

See below.

Matthew 3:3

3 γάρ ἐστιν ὁ ῥηθεὶς ὑπὸ Ἠσαΐου τοῦ προφήτου, λέγοντος,
  For is   he spoken of by Isaiah the prophet, saying.
Φωνὴ βοῶντος ἐν τῇ ἐρήμῳ, Ἑτοιμάσατε τὴν ὁδὸν Κυρίου·
  A voice of (one) crying in the wilderness: Prepare the way of (the) Lord:
4 εὐθείας ποιεῖτε τὰς τρίβους αὐτοῦ. αὐτὸς δὲ ὁ Ἰωάννης εἶχε
  straight make the paths of Him, he Now, John, had

KJV: ....For this is he that was spoken of by the prophet Esaias, saying, The voice of one crying in the wilderness, Prepare ye the way of the Lord, make his paths straight.

MKJV: .....For this is he who was spoken of by the prophet Isaiah, saying, "The voice of one crying in the wilderness: Prepare the way of [the] Lord, make His paths straight."

ERV: ....☒ ☒ [John the Baptizer] is the [one] that Isaiah the prophet was talking about: " ☒ ☒ ☒ ☒ [There is a person] shouting in the desert; Prepare the way [for the] Lord; make his paths straight."

NIV: ....This is he who was spoken of through the prophet Isaiah, ☒ "A voice of one calling in the desert, Prepare the way [for] the Lord, make straight paths for him."

NASB: .....For this is the one referred to by Isaiah the prophet, saying, "The voice of one crying in the wilderness, Make ready the Way of the LORD, Make His paths straight!"

NRSV: ..... This is the one of whom the prophet Isaiah spoke when he said: "The voice of one crying out in the wilderness: Prepare the way of the Lord, make his paths straight."

ANALYSIS: All the versions say the way of the LORD in Isaiah (that is, Jehovah) is God the Son, the One who came in the flesh, becoming the Godman. In Matthew this prophetic utterance of Isaiah is quoted, thereby proving that the Jehovah in the OT is often Christ Jesus of the NT.

Isaiah 45:23

KJV:: .... I have sworn by myself, the word is gone out of my mouth [in] righteousness, and shall not return, That unto me every knee shall bow, every tongue shall swear.

MKJV:: .... I have sworn by Myself, the word has gone out of My mouth [in] righteousness, and shall not return, that to Me every knee shall bow, every tongue shall swear.

ERV: .... I ☒☒☒☒☒☒☒☒☒☒☒☒☒☒ [will make a promise by my own power]. [And if I promise to do something, then that promise is a command. And if I command something to happen, that thing happens. And I promise that] every [person] will bow [before me] (God). [Every] ☒☒☒☒ [person will promise to follow me].

NIV: .... By myself I have sworn, ☒ ☒ ☒ ☒ ☒ ☒ my mouth has ☒ ☒ [uttered in all integrity] [a] word ☒ [that] will not ☒ [be revoked]: ☒ [Before] me every knee will bow; [by me] every tongue will swear.

NASB: ..... I have sworn by Myself, The word has gone out of My mouth [in] righteousness and will not turn back, that to Me every knee will bow, every tongue will swear [allegiance].

NRSV: ..... By myself I have sworn, from my mouth has gone forth [in] righteousness, [a] word [that] ☒ shall not return: ☒ To me every knee shall bow, every tongue shall swear.

REB: .... By my [life] ☒ I have sworn, ☒ ☒ ☒ ☒ ☒ ☒ ☒ ☒ ☒ ☒ [I have given a promise of victory, a promise that will not be broken]; ☒ [to] me every knee will bow, [by me] every tongue will swear.

ANALYSIS: Though the language in Isaiah is relatively simple, and thus easy to translate, the new versions seem to delight in rewriting the book. And it is not for readability, either. Note that the NIV has added 12 words and also has failed to translate 11 words. Then note that the REB moves even further from the original, adding 16 words, and failing to translate 11. That this is spoken of Jehovah may be seen in the context of this verse.

11 σόμεθα τῷ βήματι τοῦ Χριστοῦ. γέγραπται γάρ, Ζῶ ἐγώ,
before the judgment seat of Christ. it has been written For, live I,
λέγει Κύριος· ὅτι ἐμοὶ κάμψει πᾶν γόνυ, καὶ πᾶσα γλῶσσα
says (the) Lord, that to Me will bow every knee, and every tongue
12 ἐξομολογήσεται τῷ Θεῷ. ἄρα οὖν ἕκαστος ἡμῶν περὶ
will confess to God. So then, each one of us concerning

KJV: ....For it is written, [As] I live, saith the Lord, every knee shall bow to me, and every tongue shall confess to God.

MKJV: .....For it is written, "[As] I live, says the Lord, every knee shall bow to Me, and every tongue shall confess to God."

ERV: ....[Yes] it is written [in the Scriptures]: ☒ ☒ ☒ ☒ ☒ ☒ "Every [person] shall bow before me; ☒ every [person] will [say that I am] God. [As surely as I live, these things will happen, says the Lord (God)]."

NIV: ....☒ It is written: "[As surely as] I live, says the Lord, every knee will bow before me; ☒ every tongue will confess to God."

REB: ....For [we read in scripture, As] I live, says the Lord, to me every knee shall bow and every tongue [acknowledge] ☒☒ God.

ANALYSIS: By comparing Isa. 45:23 and Rom. 14:11, again we see that Isaiah's Jehovah is the Christ Jesus of the NT. For in verse 21, He is called Jehovah. Then in verse 22, He says plainly: "I [am] God."

Note that the REB committee cannot see the difference between acknowledge God and the original word, confess to God. One can acknowledge a lot of people, but there is only One to whom we must confess.

Many other places attest to the fact that the Jehovah that dealt with the Israelites in the OT can be seen to have been Christ, for NT passages confirm it. Compare Exodus 17:7 with 1 Cor. 10:7. Compare Psalm 68:17, 18 with Ephesians 4:8, 10, 11.

70

INVISIBILITY

Invisibility is an attribute of God. In His spiritual form, God cannot be seen by mortal eye. Yet Abraham stood and talked with Him (Gen. 18:17); Jacob saw God face to face when he wrestled with Him (Gen. 32:20); Moses saw His back parts (Ex. 33:23); Samson's parents saw Him in the person of the Angel of the Lord (Jud. 14:22); and Isaiah plainly exclaims that he had seen Jehovah of hosts (Isa.6:5). How can this be? Now you see Him, and now you don't. Those who deny that Jesus always was, is, and ever shall be eternal God, one in essence with the Father and the Spirit, cannot explain this. They see it as a contradiction, or, at best, a paradox. Yet the explanation is simple when all the Scriptures are examined and weighed. God the Father is never said to be seen. God the Holy Spirit is seen only in the form of a dove, or as tongues of fire. But God the Son is seen in person first in human form (as when He talked with Abraham, and when He wrestled with Jacob). Then at the appointed time (Gal. 4:4) He became flesh and dwelt among us, not diminishing in the least His divine attributes, as was true when He appeared in a body before the patriarchs. Though as Man He was tired, and hungry, and suffered the trials that accompany the human condition, yet He continued to be God omnipotent, omnipresent, etc., able to assert His divine powers at any time.

---

1 John 4:12a

2316	3762	4455	2300	1437	25	240
12 Θεὸν	οὐδεὶς	πώποτε	τεθέαται·	ἐὰν	ἀγαπῶμεν	ἀλλήλους,
God	No one	ever	has beheld:	If	we love	one another,

KJV: ....No man hath seen God at any time.
MKJV: .....No one has seen God at any time.
NIV: No one has [ever] seen God ☒ ☒ ☒
NASB: No one has beheld God at any time;
NRSV: No one has [ever] seen God ☒ ☒ ☒ ;
REB: God has never been seen by anyone,

John 10:30

726	1537	5495		3962	3450	1473		3962
30 ἁρπάζειν	ἐκ	τῆς χειρὸς	τοῦ	πατρός	μου.	ἐγὼ	καὶ ὁ	πατήρ
to pluck	out of	the hand	of the	Father	of Me.	I	and the	Father
1722	2070	941	3767	3825	3037		2453	
31 ἕν	ἐσμεν.	ἐβάστασαν	οὖν	πάλιν	λίθους	οἱ	Ἰουδαῖοι	ἵνα
one	are.	took up	Therefore	again	stones	the	Jews.	that

KJV: ....I and [my] Father are one.
MKJV: .....I and the Father are one!
NIV: ....The Father and I are one.
NASB, NRSV, REB, NAB the same as the MKJV or NIV.

71

```
    2982  1166  2254      3962        714  2254  3004  846
 9  Κύριε, δεῖξον ἡμῖν τὸν πατέρα, καὶ ἀρκεῖ ἡμῖν. λέγει αὐτῷ
    Lord,  show  us   the  Father,  and it suffices us.  says  to him
    2424   5118        5510 3326/5216/ 1510   3756  1097
    ὁ Ἰησοῦς, Τοσοῦτον χρόνον μεθ' ὑμῶν εἰμι, καὶ οὐκ ἔγνωκάς
    -  Jesus,    so long  a time  with  you Am I, and  not you know
    3165 5376       3708  1691  3708        3962      4459/4771
    με, Φίλιππε ; ὁ ἑωρακὼς ἐμέ, ἑώρακε τὸν πατέρα· καὶ πῶς σὺ
    Me, Phillip?  The (one) seeing Me  has seen the  Father;  and how do you
```

KJV: ....he that hath seen me hath seen the Father;

MKJV: .....He who has seen Me has seen the Father.

NIV: ....[Anyone] who has seen me has seen the Father.

NRSV: .....Whoever has seen me has seen the Father.

NASB, REB, NAB much the same as the MKJV.

```
      3290      7121      8033     1288       8034     7592    2088
   31 יַעֲקֹב  וַיִּקְרָא  שָׁם: אֹתוֹ  וַיְבָרֶךְ  לִשְׁמִי  תִשְׁאַל  זֶה  לָמָּה
      Jacob   And       .there  him  He And    name My  you     this  Why
              called           blessed
      6440    6440     430      7200       3588   6439    4725      RN34
   שָׁם הַמָּקוֹם  פְּנִיאֵל  כִּי־רָאִיתִי  אֱלֹהִים  פָּנִים  אֶל־פָּנִים
   face  to   face  God     saw I Because  ,Peniel  place the  the
                                                              of name
              6439       5674         812      2224    5315    5337
   32 אֶת־פְּנִיאֵל  עָבַר  כַּאֲשֶׁר  הַשֶּׁמֶשׁ  וַיִּזְרַח־לוֹ : נַפְשִׁי  וַתִּנָּצֵל
      ;Penuel    he     as     sun the   upon   And    my   is and
              crossed                    him   rose   .life  delivered
```

KJV: ....And Jacob called the name of the place Peniel: for I have seen God face to face, and my life is preserved.

LITV: ....And Jacob called the name of the place Face of God, [saying], Because I saw God face to face, and my life was preserved.

MKJV: .....And Jacob called the name of the place Peniel; for I have seen God face to face, and my life is preserved.

NIV: ....So Jacob called the ☒ ☒ ☒ place Peniel, [saying, It is] because I saw God face to face, and [yet] my life was [spared].

NASB: ...... So Jacob named the place Peniel, for [he said] "I have seen God face to face, yet my life has been preserved."

NRSV, REB much the same.

20 כִּי אֶת־פָּנַי לִרְאֹת תּוּכַל לֹא וַיֹּאמֶר אַדֹּם אֶת־אֲשֶׁר

for My see to are You not He And have will I whom
  face able said mercy

21 וְנִצַּבְתָּ אִתִּי מָקוֹם הִנֵּה יְהוָה וַיֹּאמֶר וָחָי הָאָדָם לֹא־יִרְאַנִי

You And by place a Behold Jehovah And and man see can no
stand shall Me said live Me

KJV: .... And he said, Thou canst not see my face: for there shall no man see me, and live.

MKJV: ..... And He said, You cannot see My face. For there shall no man see Me and live.

NASB, NIV, NRSV much the same.

REB: .... But he [added,] My face you cannot see, for no [mortal may] see me and live.

John 1:18

18 Χριστοῦ ἐγένετο. Θεὸν οὐδεὶς ἑώρακε πώποτε· ὁ μονογενὴς
Christ came into being. God No one has seen at any time; the only-begotten
υἱός, ὁ ὢν εἰς τὸν κόλπον τοῦ πατρός, ἐκεῖνος ἐξηγήσατο.
Son, who is in the bosom of the Father, that One explains (Him).

KJV: .... No man hath seen God at any time; the only begotten Son, which is in the bosom of the Father, he hath declared [him].

LITV: .... No one has seen God at any time; the only-begotten Son, who is in the bosom of the Father, that One has revealed [Him].

MKJV: ..... No one has seen God at any time; the Only-begotten Son, who is in the bosom of the Father, He has declared [Him].

ERV: .... No man has [ever] seen God ☒ ☒ ☒. But the only ☒ Son (Jesus) ☒ is ☒ ☒ ☒ ☒ [God. He is very close to] ☒ the Father [(fn - Or, "But the only God is very close to the Father.")]

NIV: .... No one has [ever] seen God ☒ ☒ ☒ , [but] [God the One and Only,] who is ☒ ☒ ☒ ☒ [at the] Father's [side, has made [him] known.

NASB: ..... No man has seen God at any time, the only begotten [God], who is in the bosom of the Father, He has explained [Him].

NRSV: ..... No one has [ever] seen God ☒ ☒ ☒ . [It is] God [the only] Son who is [close to] ☒ ☒ ☒ the Father's heart [who] ☒ ☒ has made [him] known.

REB: .... No one has [ever] seen God ☒ ☒ ☒; God's [only] Son, [he] who is [nearest to] ☒ ☒ ☒ the Father's heart, ☒ ☒ has made [him] known.

NAB: .... No one has [ever] seen God ☒ ☒ ☒ . The [only] Son, [God], who is [at] the Father's [side], ☒ ☒ has revealed [him].

CEV: .... No one has [ever] seen God. The [only] Son, [who is truly God and] is [closest to] the Father, has shown [us what God is like].

The ERV has two footnotes, saying: Some Greek copies say, ["But the only Son is very close to the Father."]) [And the Son has shown us what God is like].

73

ANALYSIS: The patristic fathers were insistent upon calling Jesus God. The Gnostic opponents were intent on depicting Jesus as a created Being, an inferior god. John 1 became a battleground because of the many references to Christ as God. Burgon says that the Gnostic Valentinus (c. 150 A.D.) devised the clever theory that the Word and the Son of God were not the same person. The Word, according to the Gnostics, was created to be the "artificer", the creator to do the things that God has planned, implanting in Him the germ of all things. The Gnostics said that Christ was 'the Beginning,' the first of God's creation, and Valentinus referred to Him as 'the Only-begotten God' and said that He was the entire essence of all the subsequent worlds (Aeons). In their lexicon, the Word was a god (and the Mormons still refer to Christ as 'a god').

The NASB follows p66, p75, Aleph, B, C*, L and 33, and puts "Only begotten God" in the text. The NAB has both the Son and God. The others seize on only-begotten to make their changes. And admittedly, the patristic fathers at times used the expression "only begotten God" (Burgon says Irenaeus did so twice, but four times as Son; yet note carefully that NU unequivocably claims Irenaeus for only-begotten God, leaving the impression that this important patristic witness did not recognize only-begotten Son as authentic Scripture! Since Irenaeus used "only-begotten Son" four times, and "only-begotten God" twice, why not use the NU tactic and claim that he favored "only-begotten Son" as God-breathed? Burgon states that Theodotus of the second century is the first to quote John 1:18, and he quotes it as we know it from the vast majority of the mss.; but others often used the term "only-begotten God" interchangeably with "only-begotten Son". John Gill opines that if "only-begotten God" is to be used, it should be punctuated the "only Begotten, God", with which Leon Morris agrees.

But all this is keeping out of sight the fact that only seven Egyptian mss. have only-begotten God, and 2,000 ms. have only-begotten Son. The critics put their trust in Egypt. Is it not more logical to put trust in the rest of Christendom where only-begotten Son appears in every manuscript all over the habitable world?

The logical conclusion from common use of language is that God is eternal, and therefore God cannot be begotten. Morris and others contend that monogenes by etymology does not refer to begetting, but to a unique relationship. The bottom line, however, as always, is the undeniable fact that only 7 manuscripts created in Egypt, out of thousands of manuscripts and lectionaries, have the words preferred by the Gnostics, the Arians later, the Socinians, the Unitarians, Mormons and Jehovah's Witnesses in our day.

The critical apparatus of the United Bible Society 'Text', after citing the Egyptian manuscripts above, also lists as 'authorities' Valentinius, Clement, Origen (all three of them Gnostics who believed Christ was a created being), Arius (who said that Christ was created before the beginning of the world), and Theodotus. But they are mistaken in Theodotus, who quoted it as the vast majority of manuscripts have it. Can a case be strong when one has to find its evidence in a handful of Gnostic-influenced manuscripts, then reinforced only by Gnostic and non-Trinitarian authors?

John 5:37

```
     1700/3754  3962  3165  649          3992/3165/3962
37  ἐμοῦ ὅτι ὁ πατήρ με ἀπέσταλκε. καὶ ὁ πέμψας με πατήρ.
    Me, that the Father  Me   has sent. And He having sent Me, (the) Father,
    848    3140       4012 1700 3777 5455,   848      191
    αὐτὸς μεμαρτύρηκε περὶ ἐμοῦ. οὔτε φωνὴν αὐτοῦ ἀκηκόατε
    He     has witnessed concerning Me, Neither the voice of Him have you heard
     4456   3777 1491 848      3708            3056     848
38  πώποτε, οὔτε εἶδος αὐτοῦ ἑωράκατε. καὶ τὸν λόγον αὐτοῦ
    at any time, nor   form   His  have you seen. And the word   of Him
```

KJV: ....And the Father himself, which hath sent me, hath borne witness of me. Ye have neither heard his voice at any time, nor seen his shape.

MKJV: .....And He sending Me, the Father Himself, has borne witness of Me. Neither have you heard His voice at any time nor seen His shape.

ERV: ....And the Father ⊠ that sent me has [given proof about] me [himself]. [But] you have never heard his voice ⊠ ⊠ ⊠. [You have] never seen [what he looks like].

NIV: ....And ⊠ the Father who sent me has himself testified [concerning] me. You have never heard his voice ⊠ ⊠ ⊠ nor seen his form.

NASB, NRSV, REB, NAB much the same.

Colossians 1:15

```
    129     848        859          266    3739/2076 1504
15  αἵματος αὐτοῦ, τὴν ἄφεσιν τῶν ἁμαρτιῶν· ὅς ἐστιν εἰκὼν
    blood   of Him, the forgiveness   of sins;   who   is (the) image
      2316     517    4416        3956   2937    3754
16  τοῦ Θεοῦ τοῦ ἀοράτου, πρωτότοκος πάσης κτίσεως· ὅτι
    of God  the   invisible, (the) firstborn  of  all    creation, because
```

KJV: ....Who is the image of the invisible God, the firstborn of every creature:

MKJV: .....who is the image of the invisible God, the Firstborn of all creation.

ERV: ....[No person can see God. But Jesus] ⊠ ⊠ ⊠ ⊠ ⊠ ⊠ ⊠ [is exactly like God]. [Jesus is ruler over all the things that have been made.]

NIV: ....⊠ [He] is the image of the invisible God, the firstborn [over] all creation.

NASB: .....[And He] is the image of the invisible God, the first-born of all creation.

NRSV: .....[He is] the image of the invisible God, the firstborn of all creation.

REB: ....[He is] the image of the invisible God, [his is the primacy over] all creation.

CEV: ....[Christ] ⊠ is [exactly like] ⊠ ⊠ ⊠ ⊠ ⊠ God, [who cannot be seen. He is] the first-born [Son], ⊠ [superior to] all creation.

5 וָאֹמַר אוֹי־לִי כִי־נִדְמֵיתִי כִּי אִישׁ טְמֵא

unclean   a   for   am I   for   to Woe I Then   smoke was   the and
of man   .off cut   ,me   said   with filled   house

שְׂפָתַיִם אָנֹכִי וּבְתוֹךְ עַם־טְמֵא שְׂפָתַיִם אָנֹכִי יֹשֵׁב כִּי אֶת־

for ,live   I   lips   unclean a   and ,(am) I   lips
of people amongst

6 הַמֶּלֶךְ יְהוָה צְבָאוֹת רָאוּ עֵינָי: וַיָּעַף אֵלַי אֶחָד מִן־הַשְּׂרָפִים

the   of   one   to   Then   my   have   ,hosts   Jehovah   the
seraphim   me   flew _eyes   seen   of   ,King

KJV: .... Then said I, Woe [is] me! for I am undone; because I [am] a man of
unclean lips, and I dwell in the midst of a people of unclean lips: for
mine eyes have seen the King, the LORD of hosts.

MKJV: ..... Then I said, Woe [is] me! For I am undone; for I [am] a man of
unclean lips, and I dwell in the midst of a people of unclean lips; for
my eyes have seen the King, Jehovah of hosts.

ERV: .... [I became very scared], ☒ I said, ["Oh, no! I will be destroyed]. ☒ I am
not pure (good) enough to speak to God]. And I live among people [that
are not pure enough to speak to God]. ☒ [Yet] I have seen the King,
the Lord [All-Powerful]."

NIV: .... Woe [to] me, ☒ I cried. ☒ I am ruined! For I [am] a man of unclean
lips, and I live among a people of unclean lips, and my eyes have seen
the King, the LORD [Almighty].

NASB, NRSV, REB, NAB much the same as the MKJV.

---

41 καρδίαν· ἵνα μὴ ἴδωσι τοῖς ὀφθαλμοῖς, καὶ νοήσωσι τῇ

heart,   that not they might see with the eyes,   and   understand with
καρδίᾳ, καὶ ἐπιστραφῶσι, καὶ ἰάσωμαι αὐτούς. ταῦτα εἶπεν

heart,   and   be converted,   and I should heal them. These things said
Ἡσαΐας, ὅτε εἶδε τὴν δόξαν αὐτοῦ, καὶ ἐλάλησε περὶ αὐτοῦ.

Isaiah   when he saw the glory of Him,   and   spoke   about   Him.

KJV: .... These things said Esaias, when he saw his glory, and spake of him.

MKJV: ..... Isaiah said these things when he saw His glory and spoke of Him.

ERV: .... Isaiah said this because he saw his (Jesus') glory. So Isaiah spoke about
him (Jesus).

NIV: .... Isaiah said [this] because he saw [Jesus'] glory and spoke [about] him.

NASB, NRSV, REB, NAB much the same as the MKJV.

ANALYSIS OF THE ABOVE VERSES: Being one in essence with the other
Persons of the Trinity (See analysis at Hebrews 1:3 above), Jesus Christ
had the attributes to exactly reveal the Father (Matt. 11:27), because He
and the Father were One (John 10:30). Why didn't the heretics tamper
with these verses, as they did with others? Perhaps they thought them
paradoxical, and therefore unconvincing. The newest versions do not
hesitate to add and subtract words, tailoring the verses to their own
understanding. See the ERV and CEV on Colossians 1:15 and John
1:18 above.

ASCENSION

Mark 16:19

```
      3303/3767/ 2962  3326        2980      846      353        1619
19  'Ο  μὲν  οὖν  Κύριος,  μετὰ  τὸ  λαλῆσαι  αὐτοῖς,  ἀνελήφθη  εἰς
    The  indeed  then  Lord,  after  the  speaking  to them, was taken up into
      3772        2523    1537  1188          2316    1565
20  τὸν  οὐρανόν,  καὶ  ἐκάθισεν  ἐκ  δεξιῶν  τοῦ  Θεοῦ.  ἐκεῖνοι  δὲ
    Heaven,  and    sat    off (the) right    of God,  they  But
```

KJV: ....So then after the Lord had spoken unto them, he was received up into
heaven, and sat on the right hand of God.

MKJV: .....Then indeed, after speaking to them, the Lord was taken up into
Heaven and sat on [the] right hand of God.

ERV: ....☒ ☒ After [the Lord Jesus] said [these things to his followers,] he was
[carried] up into heaven. ☒ [There, Jesus] sat at the right side of God.

NIV: ....After the Lord [Jesus] had spoken to them, [he] was taken up into
heaven, and he sat at the right hand of God.

NASB: So then, when the Lord [Jesus] had spoken to them, He was received
up into heaven, and sat down at the right hand of God.

NRSV: So then the Lord [Jesus], after he had spoken to them, was taken up
into heaven and sat down at the right hand of God.

Footnotes: The ERV reports correctly: "Some early Greek manuscripts end at
verse 8." The NIV reports with a heavily loaded opinion: "The most
reliable early manuscripts and other ancient witnesses do not have
Mark 16:9-20" — but like the butcher who weighs the meat with his
thumb on the scale, they are weighing the evidence on these verses
with their subjective opinion furnishing most of the weight. The
NASB footnote says: "some of the oldest mss. do not contain vv.
9-20" — assuming that two is equal to some? How about the more
than 2,000 manuscripts that do have these verses? In another footnote,
the NASB gives a verse 21 which has NO creditable evidence at all.

The NRSV double brackets these last 12 verses. But in their footnote they
give the evidence in such a way as to confuse the reader, leaving it as
if there was much doubt about whether the verses were authentic. The
REB, though not bracketing the verses, does the same as the NRSV,
hiding the fact that every Greek manuscript in the world has Mark
16:9-20 except Codices B and Aleph.

There are only two (2) Greek manuscripts without these verses. That truly is
the only 'evidence' of any consequence that the critics can offer. The
"other ancient witnesses" they refer to are never given any weight in
other textual disputes; they are scorned by the NIV. The NRSV and
NAB print two endings to Mark, with misleading footnotes. Both say
that some (authorities, witnesses) do not have vss. 9-20 (do two mss.
add up to some?) Another says that an 'authority' ends Mark at vs. 8,
concealing the fact that this is a single Latin mss., an authority they
would scorn if it contradicted their textual opinion. The NAB is more
informative, saying that four late Greek mss. have both endings, and
saying vss. 9-20 have always been accepted as canonical. But they give
unwarranted credence to the dogged insistence of some textual critics

that Mark did not write the last twelve verses, that the original ending must have been lost. Burgon wrote an entire book to refute all this speculation, and not a soul has attempted to answer his findings.

Codex B actually testifies to the fact that these verses were before the scribe, for a blank space appears at the place in Codex B where these 12 verses should be, and it is the only blank space in the manuscript. Could the copyist have been looking at an older manuscript with these 12 verses, and though ordered not to put them in, he knew how much space to leave? The other so-called 'most reliable early manuscript', Codex Sinaiticus (Aleph) is written in one fashion until it reaches the place where these last twelve verses should be. And lo and behold! All of a sudden the letters become larger, and the words are stretched out by spaces between letters just in these last 12 verses of Mark. Was this extraordinary change due to the fact that the copyist wanted to cover up the fact that these 12 verses were missing? Other than these two doctored manuscripts, every other manuscript has Mark 16:9-20; every version has them. See Burgon's *The Last Twelve Verses of Mark*, reprinted in its entirety in *Unholy Hands on the Bible*, Vol. I.

Gordon H. Clark, the noted logician, remarked that Mark 16:9-20 is a definitive test of textual critics (and translators): If they reject Mark 16:9-20, or bracket them, or throw doubt on these twelve verses as genuine, then you may be sure that they are not willing to go by the evidence.

Since all six of the major new versions bracket, double bracket, and otherwise indicate that they do not consider Mark 16:9-20 to be original God-breathed words, this eliminates Mark's witness to the bodily ascension of the Lord Jesus Christ in those versions.

Luke 24:51

```
        5495    848      2127       846            1096 1722    2127
   51  χείρας αυτού ευλόγησεν αυτούς. και εγένετο εν τῷ ευλογείν
       hands  of Him,  He blessed  them.  And   it was,   in the blessing
        846    846      1339   575, 846        399        1519
       αυτόν αυτούς, διέστη απ' αυτών, και ανεφέρετο είς το
       (of) Him   them. He withdrew from them,  and  was carried into   —
        3772        846      4352           846,      5290
   52  ουρανόν. και αυτοί προσκυνήσαντες αυτόν, υπέστρεψαν
       Heaven. And  they   having worshiped    Him     returned
```

KJV: ....And it came to pass, while he blessed them, he was parted from them, and carried up into heaven.

MKJV: .....And it happened [as] He blessed them, He withdrew from them and was carried up into Heaven.

ERV: .... ☒ ☒ ☒ [While Jesus was] blessing them, he [was separated] from them and was carried into heaven.

NIV: .... ☒ ☒ ☒ [While] he was blessing them, he left them and was taken up into heaven.

The NASB and REB omit "and was carried up into heaven," so those two new versions do not have any proof that Christ ascended back into Heaven, having discredited Mark 16:19. The NRSV footnotes that "Other ancient authorities lack **and was carried up into heaven**." But someone will think to say, What about Acts 1:9-11? Yes, the **KIV**, **NKJV** and MKJV have this for Acts 1:9-11: "And when He had spoken these things, while they beheld, he was taken up; and a cloud received Him out of their sight. And while they looked steadfastly toward heaven as He went up, behold, two men stood by them in white apparel; Which also said, Ye men of Galilee, why stand ye gazing up into heaven? This same Jesus, which is taken up from you into heaven, shall so come in like manner as ye have seen him go into heaven" But the Greek has it in all three mentions of heaven, **the heaven.**" Jesus went up into **the** heaven into a cloud, NOT into Heaven. Then the disciples were looking up into **the** heaven, into the sky, NOT into Heaven. And so the angels said to them, "why do you stand looking up into **the** heaven", into the sky again, NOT **into Heaven!** Were mortal men given supernatural sight so that they could see right into Heaven? The Scriptures never say so.

But again someone will say, Mark 16:19 and Luke 24:51 both also have **the heaven. Why then do we translate Heaven instead of the heaven in those places?** In those two places Jesus *"was carried up into Heaven and sat down at the right hand of God."* (Mark 16:19) From other places in the Scriptures (such as Heb. 9:24, where Heaven (*ouranos*) also has the article), we learn that Jesus did indeed rise into Heaven, NOT into *the heaven*, the sky. The report in Mark and in Luke is not of the disciples witnessing Jesus going up into the sky. Rather God the Holy Spirit through Mark and Luke is witnessing that Jesus was carried up into Heaven. In Acts, however, the scene portrays the disciples looking up into the sky (proof: a cloud obscured their sight).

CONCLUSION: The NIV and NASB in Acts 1:10 and 11 actually translate "the sky" though that is technically incorrect. But then at the end of verse 11, they translate "heaven," the article preceding *ouranos* in all three places. Acts 1:9-11 cannot be used to witness to the **bodily** Ascension of Jesus **into Heaven**, but Mark 16:19 and Luke 24:51 DO witness to the bodily Ascension of Jesus **into Heaven**.

THE EVIDENCE

And what is the evidence that is the cause of all this confusion? ONLY Aleph and D of the Greek manuscripts omit these words. On the basis of two obviously corrupted manuscripts (ten different hands tried to correct the Aleph (the *Sinaiticus* Codex) — and both are honeycombed with thousands of omissions, being so poorly executed. We are not only being led to give up some God-breathed words, but ALSO to give up Luke's witness to the bodily Ascension of Christ Jesus. Add to this the fact that these same human judges consider Mark's witness to the Ascension to be without apostolic authority, and what is left to the lovers of our LORD? No other words of the Scriptures give actual witness of the bodily Ascension of Christ into Heaven. We have been robbed of words that are especially essential to the complete historical recording of that most important event, the Ascension. And they claim that their version has not affected any cardinal doctrine! Is the doctrine of the bodily Ascension of Christ not a cardinal doctrine?

Will God's saints allow them to steal God's words, doing nothing to stop the spread of this kind of erosion? Never!

```
        3397    3756  2334   3165        3825   3397      3700  3165
16      μικρὸν  καὶ   οὐ    θεωρεῖτέ    με,   καὶ πάλιν μικρὸν  καὶ   ὄψεσθέ  με,
        A little and   not you behold Me, and    again  a little and you will see Me.

        3754/1473  5217    4314       3962      2036    3767/1637
17      ὅτι ἐγὼ   ὑπάγω  πρὸς   τὸν  πατέρα.  εἶπον οὖν  ἐκ  τῶν
        because I   go      to      the   Father.   said Therefore  of  the
```

KJV: ....A little while, and ye shall not see me: and again, a little while, and ye shall see me, because I go to the Father.

MKJV: ......A little [while] and you will not see Me; and again a little [while] and you will see Me, because I go to the Father.

NIV: ....[In] a little [while] you will see me no more, and [then after] a little you will see me ☒ ☒ ☒ ☒ ☒ ☒.

NASB: .....A little [while], and you will no longer behold Me, and again a little [while], and you will see me ☒ ☒ ☒ ☒ ☒ ☒.

NRSV:......a little [while] and you will no longer see me, and again a little while and you will see me ☒ ☒ ☒ ☒ ☒ ☒.

REB: ....A little [while] and you ☒ see me no more; ☒ again ☒ ☒ ☒ you will see me ☒ ☒ ☒ ☒ ☒ ☒.

NAB: ....A little [while] and you will no longer see me, and again a little [while later] you will see me ☒ ☒ ☒ ☒ ☒ ☒.

ANALYSIS: **because I go to the Father** is omitted by the six major new versions. Whether or not the one who initiated this omission intended it as a means of denying our Lord's resurrection is not certain. But it is certain that the critics and the new versionists have deliberately left out **because I go to the Father.** The foolishness of this can be seen in the very next verse where we see the disciples repeating what Jesus had just said, and they include the six words **because I go to the Father** (in which place the critics and versionists do not question the words. If Jesus had not said those words, why is it that the disciples use those words when they are repeating what Jesus said?).

But what is the evidence: Four Egyptian uncials: Aleph,B,D,L, and one Egyptian version and one Old Latin mss. All the other uncials, every single one of the cursives, and every version except one Egyptian and one Old Latin; also every father that quotes the verse, DO have the words **because I go to the Father** in John 16:16. What are they telling us? That all the uncials except 4, 2,000+ cursives, and versions in every country besides Egypt, have falsified the Scriptures by adding these six words, **because I go to the Father?** As to the claim that two papyri also omit these words, it should be considered that the papyri (all from Egypt) do not on the whole agree with the Egyptian uncials with the exception of places of omission like this. The fact is the papyri have an entirely different cast, not agreeing with B and Aleph even 50% of the time, and actually agreeing with the majority of mss. more often.

Conversely, they are telling us that these 4 highly corrupt uncials are where we can find the God-breathed words which we depend upon for life and godliness. Yet in literally thousands of places where these same manuscripts omit words, these same critics and versionists ignore the omissions of Aleph, B, D, and L. Yes, and when those same uncials agree with the majority of manuscripts, they will at places take just one uncial and spurn the rest of their favorite mss. They deny the plenary and verbal inspiration of the Scriptures, and in the place of that comforting and assuring doctrine, they offer us their own subjective judgments.

EVERLASTING KING

Jeremiah 10:10

	7110	57 69	44 28		24 18	430		571	430		3068
10	אֶלְקַצֹף	עוֹלָם וּמֶלֶךְ		חַיִּים אֱלֹהִים הוּא אֱמֶת אֱלֹהִים				יהוה

His At / wrath | ever- / .lasting | the / king | and | ,living | the / God | He / (is) | ;true | the (is) / God | | But / Jehovah

| | | 560 | 1836 | | | 2195 | 1471 | 3557 38.08 | 776: | | 7493 |

| 11 | תֹּאמְרוּן כִּדְנָה | | : וְעַמּוֹ גוֹיִם יָכִלוּ וְלֹא־ אֶרֶץ תִּרְעַשׁ | |

shall you / say | Like | | His / .indignation | the / nations | can / endure | and / not | the / ,earth | shall / quake

KJV: ....But the LORD [is] the true God, he [is] the living God, and an everlasting king: at his wrath the earth shall tremble, and the nations shall not be able to abide his indignation.

LITV: ....But Jehovah [is] the true God; He [is] the living God and the everlasting King. At His wrath the earth shall quake, and the nations cannot endure His indignation.

MKJV: .....But the LORD [is] the true God, He [is] the living God, and the everlasting King. At His wrath the earth shall tremble, and the nations shall not be able to stand His fury.

NIV: ....But the LORD [is] the true God; he is the living God, the eternal King, [when he is angry], the earth trembles; the nations cannot endure his wrath.

NASB, NRSV, much the same as the **MKJV.**

REB: ....But the LORD [is] God [in truth, ⊠ [a] living God, [an] everlasting King. The earth quakes [under] His fury; ⊠ [no nation] can endure His wrath.

ANALYSIS: Note that the REB inserts without warrant [a] before living God. This is very pleasing to the deniers of the Godhood of Jesus Christ, for they also refer to Him as **a god.**

Revelation 19:16

	2316	3841		2192/1909	2440	1909
'16	Θεοῦ	τοῦ παντοκράτορος.	καὶ ἔχει ἐπὶ τὸ ἱμάτιον καὶ ἐπὶ τὸν

of God | Almighty. | And He has on the garment and on | the

3382 | 848 | 3686 | 1125 | 935 | 935
μηρὸν αὐτοῦ ὄνομα γεγραμμένον, Βασιλεὺς βασιλέων καὶ

thigh | of Him | a name having been written: | KING | OF KINGS. AND

2962 | 2962
Κύριος κυρίων.

LORD OF LORDS.

KJV: ....And he hath on [his] vesture and on his thigh a name written, KING OF KINGS, AND LORD OF LORDS.

MKJV: .....And He has on the garment and on His thigh a name written, KING OF KINGS AND LORD OF LORDS.

NIV: ....On his robe and on his thigh he has [this] name written: KING OF KINGS AND LORD OF LORDS.

ANALYSIS: By these two verses it can be seen that Christ is the living God and the everlasting King. It is not possible for a created being to be the Word (vs. 13), Almighty God (vs. 15), and the everlasting (2 Pet. 1:11) King of kings and Lord of lords.

CREATOR

John 1:3

```
      2316/2258   3058    3778/2258/1722/746  4314        2316     3956
  2   Θεὸς  ἦν  ὁ λόγος.  οὗτος  ἦν  ἐν  ἀρχῇ  πρὸς  τὸν  Θεόν.  πάντα
  3   God  was the Word. This One was in beginning with    God. All things
      1223  846   1096           5565   846    1096    3781/1520 1096
      δι' αὐτοῦ ἐγένετο, καὶ χωρὶς αὐτοῦ ἐγένετο οὐδὲ ἓν ὃ γέγονεν.
      through Him came into and without Him  came into not even one that came into
      1722 846   2222 being.      2222/2258  being    (thing) 444 being.
```

KJV: ....All things were made by him; and without him was not any thing made that was made.

MKJV: .....All things came into being through Him, and without Him not even one thing came into being.

ERV: ....All things [were made] through him (the Word). ☒ Nothing ☒ [was made] without him.

NIV:: ....Through Him all things [were made]; without him ☒ ☒ nothing [was made that has been made].

NASB, NRSV, REB, NAB: Same as MKJV

ANALYSIS: The NIV is very quick to change the renderings of the KJV in most verses, yet here they have chosen to retain the non-literal translation of this verse. The word *egeneto* (#1096) can be translated by made when a thing is finished, but its basic meaning is to come into existence, to begin to be. Here it obviously means came into being. As Creator, Christ brought into being things that were not; where nothing was, things came into being; not even one thing came into being except through Him.

```
      2316      517        4416          3956    2937     3754
 16  τοῦ Θεοῦ τοῦ ἀοράτου, πρωτότοκος πάσης κτίσεως· ὅτι
     of God  the   invisible, (the) firstborn  of  all   creation, because
     1722/846  2936      3956      1722    3772        1909
     ἐν αὐτῷ ἐκτίσθη τὰ πάντα, τὰ ἐν τοῖς οὐρανοῖς καὶ τὰ ἐπὶ
     in  Him were created all things, the things in the heavens and the things on
        1093       3707          517     1535   2362   1535 2963
     τῆς γῆς, τὰ ὁρατὰ καὶ τὰ ἀόρατα, εἴτε θρόνοι, εἴτε κυριό-
     the earth, the visible and the invisible, whether thrones, or lordships
         1535 746   1535 1849          3956  1223  846        1519
     τητες, εἴτε ἀρχαί, εἴτε ἐξουσίαι· τὰ πάντα δι᾽ αὐτοῦ καὶ εἰς
       or  rulers,   or authorities;  all things through  Him and for
      846    2936       846  2076/4253 3956                3956
 17  αὐτὸν ἔκτισται· καὶ αὐτός ἐστι πρὸ πάντων, καὶ τὰ πάντα
     Him have been created, and He is before all things, and   all things
```

KJV: .... For by him were all things created, that are in heaven, and that are in earth, visible and invisible, whether [they be] thrones, or dominions, or principalities, or powers: all things were created by him, and for him:

LITV: .... for all things were created in Him, the things in the heavens, and the things on the earth, the things visible, and the things invisible; whether thrones, or lordships, or rulers, or authorities, all things have been created through Him and for Him.

MKJV: ..... For all things were created in Him, the things in the heavens, and the things on the earth, the things visible and the things invisible, whether thrones or dominions or principalities or powers, all things were created through Him and for Him.

NKJV: ..... For [by] Him all things were created [that are] ☒ ☒ in ☒ heaven and [that are] on ☒ earth, ☒ ☒ visible and ☒ ☒ invisible, whether thrones or dominions or principalities or powers. All things were created through Him and for Him.

ERV: .... ☒ [Through his power] all things [that were made] - things in heaven and ☒ ☒ on earth, ☒ ☒ [things seen] and ☒ ☒ [not seen], ☒ ☒ [all spiritual powers] ☒, authorities, ☒ [lords], and ☒ rulers. All things were [made] through Christ and for ☒ [Christ].

NIV: .... For [by] him all things were created: ☒ things in ☒ [heaven] and ☒ ☒ on ☒ earth, ☒ ☒ visible and ☒ ☒ invisible, whether thrones or powers or rulers or authorities, all things were created by him and for him.

NASB: ..... For [by] Him all things were created, [both] ☒ ☒ in the heavens and ☒ ☒ on ☒ earth, ☒ ☒ visible and ☒ ☒ invisible, whether thrones or dominions or rulers or authorities — all things have been created by Him and for Him.,

NRSV: ..... for in him all things in ☒ heaven and on ☒ earth were created, ☒ things visible and ☒ ☒ invisible, whether thrones or dominions or rulers or powers — all things have been created through him and for him.

REB: .... ☒ in him everything in ☒ heaven and on ☒ earth was created, [not only] ☒ things visible [but also] the ☒ invisible ☒ [orders of] thrones, sovereignties, authorities and powers; the [whole universe has been] created through him and for him.

ANALYSIS: Although all the new versions above witness to the fact that Christ created all things, it should be noted that they have a penchant for adding to and subtracting from what the Greek says. According to Thayer, *en* (#1722) with the dative should be translated in, rather than by. Most of them ignore *ta* which is often translated "the things", as in Phil. 1:27 and elsewhere. This word *ta* appears six times in this verse, before the heavens, the earth, visible, invisible, at the beginning and again at the end, *ta panta* = all the things.

Note also that *ouranois* is plural, *the heavens*. Does this not refer to the creation of the expanse, rather than the things in Heaven? See Heb. 1:10 below.

Hebrews 1:10

```
    2316/4676  1637   20                    3844      3353    4676
10  Θεός σου, Ελαιον ἀγαλλιάσεως παρὰ τοὺς μετόχους σου. καί,
    God of You, (with) oil of gladness    above  the  partners of You. And:
    4771/2596/746   2962    1093   2311,              2041
    Σὺ κατ' ἀρχάς, Κύριε, τὴν γῆν ἐθεμελίωσας, καὶ ἔργα τῶν
    You at (the) beginning Lord, the earth  founded,    and works of the
    5495_  4676/1526   3772    846     622           4771   1265
11  χειρῶν σου εἰσιν οἱ οὐρανοί· αὐτοὶ ἀπολοῦνται, σὺ δὲ δια-
    hands of You are the heavens:  they  will perish,  You but will
```

KJV: ....And, Thou, Lord, in the beginning hast [laid the foundation] of the earth; and the heavens are the works of thine hands:

LITV: ....And, "You, Lord, at [the] beginning founded the earth, and the heavens are works of Your hands.

MKJV: ..... And, "You, Lord, have founded the earth [in the] beginning, and the heavens are the works of Your hands."

ERV: ....[God] also [says], [O] Lord, in the beginning you ☒ ☒ [made] the earth, And ☒ ☒ ☒ ☒ ☒ your hands [made the sky].

NIV: ....[He] also [says], ☒ [In the] beginning [O] Lord, you [laid the foundations] of the earth, and the heavens are the work of your hands.

NASB: ....And, Thou, LORD, ☒ [in the] beginning didst [lay the foundation] of the earth, and the heavens are [the] works of thy hands.

REB: ....And, [again], [By] you, Lord, [were] ☒ earth's [foundations laid of old], and the heavens are the work of your hands.

NRSV: .....And, ☒ [in the] beginning, Lord, you founded the earth, and the heavens are [the] work of your hands.

NAB: ....and, At the beginning, [O] Lord, you established the earth, and the heavens are [the] work[s] of your hands.

ANALYSIS: kat' archas = at [the] beginning, rather than, [in the] beginning.

................It is incorrect to translate *ethemeliosas* as **foundation**, for in the Greek it is a verb, **founded**. All versions agree that the earth and the heavens were the work of the hands of Christ, God the Son.

84

```
         421        4149       5547              5461
  9  τὸν ἀνεξιχνίαστον πλοῦτον τοῦ Χριστοῦ, καὶ φωτίσαι
     the    unsearchable    riches        of Christ, and to bring to light
     3956  5101   2842        3466              613
  πάντας τίς ἡ κοινωνία τοῦ μυστηρίου τοῦ ἀποκεκρυμμένου
     all,  what (is) the fellowship of the mystery    having been hidden
     575      165 1722       2316         3956   2936   1223
  ἀπὸ τῶν αἰώνων ἐν τῷ Θεῷ τῷ τὰ πάντα κτίσαντι διὰ
     from the   ages    in    God, the (One)   all things having through
                                                        created
     2424   5547    2443  1107    3566        746
  10 Ἰησοῦ Χριστοῦ, ἵνα γνωρισθῇ νῦν ταῖς ἀρχαῖς καὶ ταῖς
     Jesus  Christ,     that might be made known now to the rulers and to the
```

KJV: .... And to make all [men] see what [is] the fellowship of the mystery, which from the beginning of the world hath been hid in God, who created all things by Jesus Christ.

LITV: .... and to bring all to light, what [is] the stewardship of the mystery having been hidden in God from the ages, the [One] having created all things through Jesus Christ.

MKJV: ..... and to make all see what [is] the fellowship of the mystery which from the beginning of the [world] has been hidden in God, [who] created all things by Jesus Christ.

NIV: .... and make plain [to everyone] the administration of [this] mystery, which from ages [past was kept] hidden in God, [who] created all things ☒ ☒ ☒ .

NASB: ..... and to bring ☒ to light what is the administration of the mystery which for ages has been hidden in God, [who] created all things ☒ ☒ ☒ .

NRSV: ..... and to make [everyone] see ☒ what is the [plan of] the mystery hidden for ages in God [who] created all things ☒ ☒ ☒ .

REB: .... and of bringing ☒ to light [how this] hidden ☒ [purpose was to be put into effect]. ☒ ☒ ☒ ☒ [It lay] concealed [for long] ☒ ages [with] ☒ God ☒ ☒ ☒ [the Creator of the universe].

NAB: .... and to bring to light [for all] what is the ☒ ☒ mystery hidden from ages [past] in God [who] created all things ☒ ☒ ☒ .

JWV: .... and to bring ☒ to light what the house administration of the mystery [of] the [one] having been hidden away from the ages in God ☒ ☒ ☒ .

ANALYSIS: All the new versions except KJV, LITV, MKJV, NKJV omit the words **all** and **through Jesus Christ**. Why? Only Aleph, A, and two cursives omit **all**. Consider this, that between Aleph, and A in the epistles, there are thousands of omissions.

B, C, and F-G join Aleph A and D in omitting the very important God-breathed words, *through Jesus Christ*. Why do the critics and the new versions seize upon these four words to omit? Hear this from a leading critic who favors the Alexandrian mss.: "Egypt was distinguished from other provinces of the Church, so far as we can judge, by the early dominance of gnosticism; . . . (*Text of the New Testament*, Kurt Aland, p. 59). Yet it was in this Gnostic-dominated Egypt that these few omission-laced mss. were created. And it was a Gnostic tactic to remove as many proofs of the Godhood of Jesus

85

Christ as possible. That gives a credible explanation of why the words *through Jesus Christ* are missing from the Egyptian mss., the Vulgate and other Latin copies, and the two Egyptian versions, the Coptic and the Ethiopic, but it furnishes NO reason why all the new versions would use such adulterated mss. as an excuse for removing words that say that God created *through Jesus Christ*. For these words appear in thousands of manuscripts, even some that originated in Egypt.

IMMUTABILITY

Malachi 3:6

אָמַ֥ר יְהוָ֖ה צְבָא֑וֹת כִּ֚י אֲנִ֣י יְהוָ֔ה לֹ֥א שָׁנִ֖יתִי וְאַתֶּ֥ם בְּנֵֽי־ 6

sons of	and you	do xchange	not	Jehovah	I	For	.hosts	Jehovah	says of

יַעֲקֹ֖ב לֹ֥א כְלִיתֶֽם׃ לְמִימֵ֣י אֲבֹתֵיכֶ֗ם סַרְתֶּ֛ם מֵחֻקַּ֖י וְלֹ֥א 7

and not	My from statutes	have you turned	your .fathers	the From of days	come have .and an to	not	Jacob

KJV: ....For I [am] the LORD, I change not; therefore ye sons of Jacob are not consumed.

LITV: ....For I [am] Jehovah; I change not; therefore you sons of Jacob are not consumed.

Other versions virtually the same.

See below

Hebrews 13:8

8 ἀναστροφῆς, μιμεῖσθε τὴν πίστιν. Ἰησοῦς Χριστὸς χθὲς καὶ
391 3401 4102 2424 5547 5504
conduct. imitate (their) faith; Jesus Christ yesterday and
9 σήμερον ὁ αὐτός, καὶ εἰς τοὺς αἰῶνας. διδαχαῖς ποικίλαις καὶ
4594 846 1519 165 1322 4164
today (is) the same. even to the ages. teaching By various and

KJV: ....Jesus Christ the same yesterday, and today, and forever.

MKJV: .....Jesus Christ the same yesterday and today and forever.

ERV: ....Jesus Christ [is] the same yesterday, today, and forever.

NIV: ....Jesus Christ [is] the same yesterday, today, and forever.

Other versions the same.

ANALYSIS: God must be immutable, unchangeable. For if He would change for the better, it would prove that He had not been perfect; therefore He was not God. If He changed for the worse, then He would no longer be perfect, and could not be God. Then if it is true, as the Scriptures affirm, that Jesus Christ is the same yesterday, today, and forever, it proves that He is immutable, that He is God. If He is "the Alpha and the Omega, the Beginning and the Ending, the First and the Last, and He has always been the same, and will be forever, from eternity past to eternity future (Rev. 1:8, 11, 17), then He must be God. For those things cannot truly be said of any creature, however high or ancient that creature may be.

SUPREME JUDGE

Romans 14:10b

```
   2198      2961      4771 5101   2919        80      4676 2228
10 ζώντων κυριεύσῃ. σὺ δὲ τί κρίνεις τὸν ἀδελφόν σου ; ἢ καὶ
   of living He might be Lord. you And why judge the brother of you? Or also
4771/5101/ 1848          80      4675  3956    1063    3936
σὺ τί ἐξουθενεῖς τὸν ἀδελφόν σου ; πάντες γὰρ παραστη-
you why despise    the    brother of you?  all      For     shall stand
                 968      5547           1125        1063/2198/1473
11 σόμεθα τῷ βήματι τοῦ Χριστοῦ. γέγραπται γάρ, Ζῶ ἐγώ,
   before the judgment seat   of Christ. It has been written For, live I.
```

KJV: ....for we shall all stand before the judgment seat of Christ.

MKJV: ......For all shall stand before the judgment seat of Christ.

NIV: ....For [we] all shall stand before [God's] judgment seat ⊠ ⊠.

NASB: ......For [we] all shall stand before the judgment seat of ⊠ [God].

NRSV: ......For [we] will all stand before the judgment seat of ⊠ [God].

REB: ....⊠ [we] shall all stand before ⊠ ⊠ ⊠ ⊠ ⊠[God's tribunal].

NAB: ....For [we shall] all stand before the judgment seat of [God].

GNB: ....All [of us] shall stand before ⊠ ⊠ ⊠ ⊠ ⊠ [God to be judged by him].

CEV: ....⊠ ⊠ ⊠ ⊠ ⊠ ⊠ ⊠ ⊠ [The day is coming when God will judge] all [of us].

JWV: ....For [we] shall all stand ⊠ ⊠ ⊠ ⊠ alongside [to the step of the God].

ANALYSIS: The evidence for God, per Leon Morris (Romans, p. 483), Aleph (but not the original hand); A, B, C, D, G (9th cent. mss.). The evidence for Christ, per Morris, Aleph (not the original hand, nor are we told what the original hand wrote), P, Psi. To which Morris appends, "and others," but he does not say as he should, "and all others." Since there are no less than ten correctors of Aleph, and none of them known, what is the value of such a corrupted mss.? And as for C, it was so little thought of that someone simply blanched it so that something else could be written over it. Nothing is said about what the versions or the fathers have said on this verse. But Morris gives us his judgment: "The weight of the MSS. is behind theou, and it would seem that Christou has been imported from 2 Cor. 5:10." (ibid.)

Apparently, it has proven a successful ploy to slide by a deletion of Jesus Christ in such a way, giving only enough of the evidence to make it look like the mss. for "God" outweigh, or at least are older than, those for "Christ".

And to provide the grease to ease off the subject, a suggestion is made that "it would seem to be an importation from 2 Cor. 5:10." There is not a bit of evidence that anyone imported *of Christ* from 2 Cor. 5:10. But look at it this way, in 2 Cor. 5:10 we read "the judgment seat of Christ," the very same words we read here. Elsewhere in many places we read that it is Christ who will sit on the great white throne and judge all that stand before it (Rev. 20:11; see also 2 Tim. 4:1; Matt. 25:31; Acts 10:42; 17:41; Heb. 1:8). And since we do not read of the "judgment seat of God" anywhere but in those corrupt Egyptian mss., and since hundreds of mss. from all over Christendom have *the judgment seat of Christ* here in Romans 14:10, should it not seem right to conclude that the vast majority of mss. are correct in saying the **judgment seat of Christ?** Also it would seem that this was just another attempt of the heretics to remove testimony that Christ is the supreme Judge of humanity, that being His assigned role in the Trinity. Why didn't they remove Christ's name from all other places? It is very unlikely that those who made these fraudulent changes had the opportunity to tamper with the entire NT. Or, perhaps, the wily Serpent thought it enough to create confusion and contradiction within the Scriptures, depending on foolish men like our critics to take the bait of the altered manuscripts.

Conclusion: Do not be led astray by these new versions, for you and I will certainly appear before the **judgment seat of Christ!**

Note the way the GNB, CEV, and JWV feel free to completely misrepresent what God breathed out in this verse. It is obvious that they have no love for God's Word as it was written, but only love what they think it ought to say.

Isaiah 53:11

	7648	7200	53.15	5999	16743	3027	30.68	2656	3117

יָמִים וְחֵפֶץ יְהוָה בְּיָדוֹ יִצְלָח : מֵעֲמַל נַפְשׁוֹ יִרְאֶה יִשְׂבָּע 11

shall He	shall He	His	the Of	· shall	His in	Jehovah	the and	days
.satisfied be	see	soul	of travail	.prosper	hand		of pleasure	

54.45	5771	7227	6660	6662	6663	.1847

בְּדַעְתּוֹ יַצְדִּיק צַדִּיק עַבְדִּי לָרַבִּים וַעֲוֹנֹתָם הוּא יִסְבֹּל :

shall	He	their and	,many for	My	righteous	shall	His By
.bear		iniquities		servant		justify	knowledge

KJV: ....He shall see of the travail of his soul, [and] shall be satisfied: by his knowledge shall my righteous servant justify many; for he shall bear their iniquities.

MKJV: .....He shall see [the fruit] of the travail of His soul. He shall be fully satisfied. By His knowledge shall My righteous servant justify for many, and He shall bear their iniquities.

NIV: [After] the suffering of his soul, he will see the ☒ [light of life], and be satisfied; by his knowledge my righteous servant will justify ☒ many, and he will bear their iniquities.

NASB: [As a result] of the anguish of His soul, He will see [it] and be satisfied; By His knowledge [the] Righteous [One], My Servant, will justify ☒ the many, [As] He will bear their iniquities.

NRSV: [Out] of his anguish ☒☒☒ he shall see [light]; he shall [find satisfaction] through his knowledge. The righteous one, my servant, shall ☒☒ [make] many [righteous], and he shall bear their iniquities

REB: [By] ☒ his ☒ [humiliation] my ☒ servant will justify ☒ many; ☒ [after] his suffering he will see ☒ ☒ ☒ [light and] ☒ ☒ be satisfied; [it is their guilt] ☒ he ☒ ☒ ☒ [bears] ☒ ☒.

ANALYSIS: Note above how the new versions rob Christ of the travail of his soul. Also note that they have Him justify many instead of justify for many. And by changing the order of the words all around, they make it virtually impossible to know what God has promised in this verse.

Then note below how the new versions contradict the sure promises embedded in Isa. 53:11:

21 πάσχοντες ὑπομενεῖτε, τοῦτο χάρις παρὰ Θεῷ. εἰς τοῦτο
γὰρ ἐκλήθητε, ὅτι καὶ Χριστὸς ἔπαθεν ὑπὲρ ἡμῶν, ἡμῖν
ὑπολιμπάνων ὑπογραμμόν. ἵνα ἐπακολουθήσητε τοῖς

22 ἴχνεσιν αὐτοῦ· ὃς ἁμαρτίαν οὐκ ἐποίησεν, οὐδὲ εὑρέθη δόλος

KJV: .... For even hereunto were ye called: because Christ also suffered for us, leaving us an example, that ye should follow his steps:

LITV: .... For were you not called to this? For Christ also suffered on behalf of us, leaving us an example, that you should follow His steps.

ERV: .... [That is what you] were ☒ ☒ ☒ called [to do]. ☒ Christ ☒ ☒ ☒ ☒ ☒, ☒ ☒ [gave you] an example [to] ☒ follow You should ☒ ☒ [do the same as He did].

NIV: .... ☒ To this you were ☒ called because Christ ☒ suffered for [you], leaving [you] an example, that [you] should follow [in] His steps.

NASB: ..... For you have been called for this purpose [since] Christ also suffered for [you], leaving you an example for you to follow in His steps.

NRSV: ..... For to this you have been called, because Christ also suffered for [you], leaving you an example, so that you should follow in his steps.

REB: .... [It is your vocation because] Christ [Himself] suffered on [your] behalf, and left you an example in order that you should follow in His steps.

NAB: .... For to this you have been called because Christ has suffered for [you], leaving you an example that you should follow in His footsteps.

ANALYSIS: GNB, CEV, and JWV, as well as the versions above, all have Christ suffering for you instead of suffering for us.

The YOU could be anybody and everybody; the US could be only the elect. Again we have universal salvation being taught. The apostle Peter was being "borne along by the Holy Spirit" (2 Pet. 1:21) to give us the joy and comfort which derives from knowing that Christ, "who Himself bore in His body our sins onto the Tree, that having died to sins we might live to righteousness" (1 Peter 2:24, just below this verse. Now who is it that the Holy Spirit is saying that Christ suffered for? It is us, the ones whose sins He bore in His body on the Cross!

Many manuscripts have you, instead of us in this verse. Perhaps this is due to the close similarity of the two Greek words: *hmin* = us; *umon* = you. for there are a number of places where these words are interchanged. Again you see that the Egyptian manuscripts, p72, Aleph, A, B, furnish the reason for the critics and the new versionists to introduce the confusion caused by having verse 21 read you, your, and verse 24 read our.

47 3778 3708 3962 281 281 3004 4213 4100
οὗτος ἑώρακε τὸν πατέρα. ἀμὴν ἀμὴν λέγω ὑμῖν, ὁ πιστεύων
this One has seen the Father.   Truly, truly, I say to you, he believing
1519/1691/2192/2222 166   1473 / 1510   740   2222
48 εἰς ἐμέ, ἔχει ζωὴν αἰώνιον. ἐγώ εἰμι ὁ ἄρτος τῆς ζωῆς. οἱ
49 in Me has life everlasting. I am the bread — of life. The

KJV: ....Verily, verily, I say unto you, He that believeth on me hath everlasting life.
LITV: ....Truly, truly, I say to you, the [one] believing into Me has life everlasting.
MKJV: ......Truly, truly, I say to you, he who believes [on] Me has everlasting life.
ERV: ....I tell you [the] truth. [If a person] believes ☒ ☒ , [then that person] has life forever.
NIV:: ....I tell you [the] truth, he who believes ☒ ☒ has everlasting life.
NASB: ......Truly, truly, I say to you, he who believes ☒|☒ has eternal life.
NRSV: ......Very truly, I [tell] ☒ ☒ you, whoever believes ☒|☒ has eternal life.
REB: ....[In very truth] I [tell] you, whoever believes ☒|☒ has eternal life.
GNB: ....I [tell] you [the truth, he who believes ☒|☒ has eternal life.
CEV: ....I [tell] you [for certain] that [everyone who has faith] in me has eternal life.
JWV: ....Amen, Amen, I [am saying] to you, the [one] believing ☒|☒ is having life everlasting.

ANALYSIS: Not only the ERV and NIV omit into Me, but also the NASB, REB, NRSV, GNB, NAB and JWV, thus teaching the false doctrine that one does not have to believe into Jesus in order to have everlasting life. This is a flat denial of the Gospel. The CEV does have in Me, though 7 of their 15 words do not meet the Greek. What a pleasing message these new versions give unbelieving, disobedient sinners, saying: Believe and you will have eternal life!

Note how everyone of these skewed versions prefer eternal life to everlasting life. The reason escapes most readers. But it is fashionable to say eternal life instead of everlasting life. It began among the liberal and modernist theologians, who had some hidden purpose behind the change. But in this century it has become politically correct even among the so-called conservative theologians, translators, etc. to say eternal life. Dean Burgon says that this total change from *everlasting* to *eternal* was introduced by unbelievers. Can we count on it as a telltale sign to reveal to us who we should travel with? Well, maybe not, but just the same when you see everlasting turned into eternal in virtually every place in the Bible, pause and consider.

EVIDENCE: To whom do we owe this radical change in the basis for salvation and everlasting life? For the new versions promise everlasting life to everyone who believes. But the Greek in the vast majority of manuscripts promises everlasting life only to the persons who believe in Christ.

For eternal life without believing in Christ; p66, Aleph, B, C, L, T,and W, and a few later cursives.

For everlasting life by believing INTO CHRIST: Every other Greek manuscript in the ratio of 99 to 1, executed in various parts of the habitable world.

For me and my house, we will believe into Christ because we know that there is no other salvation except through Him.

```
     2220      1571        3767        3820      2219  2443/5600/3601
7  ζυμοι ;  ἐκκαθάρατε  οὖν  τὴν  παλαιὰν  ζύμην,  ἵνα  ἦτε  νέον
   leavens?  purge out   Then  the    old     leaven,   that you be a new
     5446   2531   2075  106        1063        3957   2267  5228
   φύραμα, καθώς ἐστε ἄζυμοι, καὶ γὰρ τὸ πάσχα ἡμῶν ὑπέρ
   lump,   ■  you are unleavened, also For the Passover of us   for
    2257   2380     5547     5620    1858          3361/1722/2219  3820
8  ἡμῶν ἐθύθη Χριστός·  ὥστε ἑορτάζωμεν, μὴ ἐν ζύμῃ παλαιᾷ,
   us was sacrificed, Christ,  so as  let us keep feast, not with leaven  old.
```

KJV: ....Purge out therefore the old leaven, that ye may be a new lump, as ye are unleavened. For even Christ our passover is sacrificed for us:

LITV: ......Then purge out the old leaven so that you may be a new lump, even as you are unleavened. For also Christ our Passover was sacrificed for us.

MKJV: .....Therefore purge out the old leaven so that you may be a new lump, as you are unleavened. For also Christ our Passover is sacrificed for us.

ERV: ....⊠ Take out [all] the old ⊠ [yeast] (sin), so that you [will] be a new ⊠ [batch of dough]. ⊠ ⊠ ⊠ ⊠ [You really are Passover bread without yeast]. [Yes], Christ, our Passover ⊠ ⊠ [lamb has already been killed] ⊠ ⊠.

NIV: ....⊠ [Get rid of] ⊠⊠ the old ⊠ [yeast] that you may be a new ⊠ [batch without yeast] — as you [really] are ⊠. For ⊠ Christ, our Passover lamb, has been sacrificed ⊠ ⊠

NASB: .....⊠ Clean out the old leaven, that you may be a new lump, just as you are [in fact] unleavened. For Christ our Passover has been sacrificed ⊠ ⊠ .

NRSV: .....⊠ Clean out the old ⊠ [yeast] so that you may be a new ⊠ [batch], as you [really] are unleavened. For our paschal lamb, Christ, has been sacrificed ⊠ ⊠ .

REB: ....⊠ [Get rid of] ⊠ ⊠ the old leaven [and then] you [will] be a new ⊠⊠⊠ [batch of] unleavened [dough]. [Indeed] you [already] are, because Christ our Passover lamb has been sacrificed ⊠ ⊠ .

GNB: ....⊠ [You must] take out [this] old ⊠ [yeast of sin] so that you [will] be ⊠⊠⊠⊠⊠⊠ [entirely pure. Then] you [will] be like a new [batch of dough]. For our Passover feast [is ready, now that] Christ, our Passover lamb, has been sacrificed ⊠ ⊠.

NAB: ....⊠ Clear out the old ⊠ [yeast], so that you may become a fresh ⊠ [batch of dough], inasmuch as you are unleavened. For our paschal lamb, Christ, has been sacrificed ⊠ ⊠.

ANALYSIS: By fermentation, **yeast** causes bread to rise. By fermentation, **leaven** causes bread to rise. But leaven is not yeast, and yeast is not a translation of #2219. It follows that being **without yeast** is not a true translation of the word which means unleavened. Leaven was a lump of dough kept over from day to day and used to leaven a batch of dough, but it is not true translation to put batch of dough as a translation for lump. The Greek word pascha is from a Hebrew word meaning to pass over. Here it is a noun, and can mean Passover, paschal lamb, or paschal feast. Since the words "Christ our Passover" is a good translation, one embedded in the theological language of the

93

ages, it seems senseless to try to use any other translation for the word. Is this not simply a change made for the sake of change?

But the most important change the new versions have made in this verse is occasioned by their deleting those precious words for us. A sacrifice is made for a purpose. For what purpose was Christ sacrificed? The original passover sacrifice was made for a specific group of people. The same is true of the sacrifice of Christ, it was made for a specific group of people, for us, for a certain select people chosen before the foundation of the world (Eph. 1:4; 1 Pet. 1:20). Merely to say that He was sacrificed, as these new versions do, is meaningless unless they are assuming that Christ's sacrifice was for the whole human race. If that were true, (1) then either every person will be delivered from the penalty of their sins, or, (2) the sacrifice of Christ by itself, without augmentation, was not sufficient to save from the penalty of sin. They leave it so that the Universalists are made happy, and also that the preachers of salvation by works will be joyful.

What does this do to our Savior God's sacrifice? It makes it of doubtful value on the one hand, or it makes Him a sacrifice for the vilest of unrepentant, faithless men.

Again we see these new versionists taking the word of a handful of Egyptian manuscripts, and ignoring all the other mss. from every region of the world.

What was the sacrifice of Christ worth? In the eyes of the new versionists (in this passage at least), not much! Men may make a sacrifice without accomplishing anything. But when Christ sacrificed Himself, it accomplished all His purposes, including the remission of all the sins of all the elect, those He chose before the foundation of the world.

1
5547   3767   3958   5228 2257 4561   5210
Χριστοῦ οὖν παθόντος ὑπὲρ ἡμῶν σαρκί, καὶ ὑμεῖς τὴν
Christ Therefore having suffered for us in (the) flesh, also you the
846   1771   3695   3754   3958 1722 456)   3973
αὐτὴν ἔννοιαν ὁπλίσασθε· ὅτι ὁ παθὼν ἐν σαρκί, πέπαυται
same   mind arm yourselves, because he suffering in (the) flesh has ceased
266   1519   3371   444   1939   235   2307

2
ἁμαρτίας· εἰς τὸ μηκέτι ἀνθρώπων ἐπιθυμίαις, ἀλλὰ θελή-
from sin: for the no longer   of men   in (the) lusts. but in (the) will

KJV: ....Forasmuch then as Christ hath suffered for us in the flesh, arm
yourselves likewise with the same mind: for he that hath suffered in the
flesh hath ceased from sin;

MKJV: ......Since then Christ has suffered for us in [the] flesh, also you arm
yourselves [with] the same thought, because he suffering in [the] flesh
has ceased from sin.

ERV: ....☒ ☒ Christ ☒ suffered ☒ ☒ [while he was] in ☒☒ [his body]. ☒
[So] you should strengthen yourselves [with] the same ☒ [kind of
thinking Christ had]. [The person] who has suffered in [his body] is
finished [with] sin.

NIV: ......☒ ☒ Christ suffered ☒ ☒ [while] in [the body]. ☒ [So] you should
[strengthen] yourselves [with] the same ☒ [kind of thinking Christ
had]. [The person who] ☒ has suffered in [his body] is finished [with]
sin.

NASB: .....Therefore, since Christ has suffered ☒ ☒ in the flesh, arm yourselves
also with the same [purpose], because he who has suffered in the flesh
has ceased from sin.

NRSV: .....Since therefore Christ suffered ☒ ☒ in the flesh, arm yourselves also
with the same intention (for [whoever] has ☒ suffered in the flesh has
finished [with] ☒ sin).

REB: ....☒ Since Christ [endured bodily] suffering ☒ ☒, you also must arm
yourselves with the same [disposition]. [When anyone has endured
bodily] ☒ suffering he ☒☒☒ has finished [with] sin.

NAB: ....Therefore, since Christ suffered ☒ ☒ in the flesh, arm yourselves also
with the same [attitude] (for [whoever] suffers in the flesh has [broken
with] sin).

The NIV, NASB, NRSV, EWV, GNB, CEV, and JWV all report that Christ
suffered in [the] flesh, but NOT for us. So in these versions there is no
apparent reason for Christ's suffering. Though all the world should
agree to make Christ's suffering and sacrifice only general, we will
remember that God has preserved for us a plentiful witness that it was
for us that He lived, died and rose again.

EVIDENCE: p72, B, C, Psi, and a few late mss. omit for us. The new
versionists are again following Codex B (c. 325 A.D.). But B also says
that there was an eclipse when the moon was 180 degrees from the sun,
an impossible astronomical absurdity (Luke 23:45). Why, then, should
we believe these few mss. against all others when they deny that Christ
died for us? If Christ did not die for us, then we are of all men most
miserable, being without hope and without God (Eph. 2:12).

Will our hope be blasted by a handful of adulterated Egyptian manuscripts
created in Gnostic-dominated Egypt? Certainly not! For the truth that
Christ suffered for us, an elect people, is embedded in the Scriptures
from Genesis to Revelation.

95

```
     1722      5124  3361/ 2990        5209      27          3754  3391
8   'Εν  δὲ τοῦτο μὴ λανθανέτω ὑμᾶς, ἀγαπητοί, ὅτι μία
    one But this thing not let be hidden from you, beloved,    that one
     2250   3844    2962/5613/5507/2094            5507/2094/5613/2250
    ἡμέρα παρὰ Κυρίῳ ὡς χίλια ἔτη, καὶ χίλια ἔτη ὡς ἡμέρα
    day    with (the) Lord (is) as a thousand and a thousand    as   day
     3391/3756  1019      2962    years  1860      years  5100   1022
9   μία. οὐ βραδύνει ὁ Κύριος τῆς ἐπαγγελίας, ὡς τινές βραδύ-
    one. not is slow The Lord of the promise,       as some slowness
           2233     236   3114    1519/2248/3361 1014
    τῆτα ἡγοῦνται· ἀλλὰ μακροθυμεῖ εἰς ἡμᾶς, μὴ βουλόμενός
           deem,    but is long-suffering toward us, not having purposed
    5100    622    235   3956   1519    3341      5562
    τινας ἀπολέσθαι, ἀλλὰ πάντας εἰς μετάνοιαν χωρῆσαι.
    any    to perish,  but  all    to repentance to come.
```

KJV: ....But, beloved, be not ignorant of this one thing, that one day [is] with the Lord as a thousand years, and a thousand years as one day. The Lord is not slack concerning his promise, as some men count slackness; but is longsuffering to us-ward, not willing that any should perish, but that all should come to repentance.

MKJV: .....But, Beloved, let not this one thing be hidden [from] you, that one day is with the Lord as a thousand years, and a thousand years as one day. The Lord is not slow [concerning His] promise, as some men count slowness, but is longsuffering to us, not having purposed that any [of us] should perish, but that all [of us] should come to repentance.

ERV: ....But ☒ [don't forget] this one thing ☒☒, [dear friends]: [to] the Lord, a day [is] like a thousand years, and a thousand years like [a] day. The Lord is not slow [in doing what] he promised — [the way] ☒ some ☒☒ [people understand] slowness. ☒☒☒☒☒☒ [God] did not want any [person] to be lost. ☒☒☒☒☒☒☒ [God wants every person to change his heart and stop sinning].

NIV: ....But [do not forget] this one thing ☒ ☒ ☒ ☒ , [dear friends]: With [the] Lord [a] day is like a thousand years, and a thousand years [are] like [a] day. [The Lord] is not slow ☒ [in keeping his] promise, as some ☒☒ [understand] slowness. ☒ [He] is patient ☒ ☒ [with you], not [wanting] ☒ any[one] to perish, but ☒☒ [everyone] to come to repentance.

NASB: .....But do not let this one [fact escape your notice], beloved, that with the Lord one day is as a thousand years, and a thousand years as one day. The Lord is not slow about His promise, as some count slowness, but is patient toward ☒ [you], not [wishing] for any to perish but for all to come to repentance.

NRSV: .....But ☒☒☒☒☒☒ [do not ignore the fact], beloved, that with the Lord one day is like a thousand years, and a thousand years are like one day. The Lord is not slow about his promise, as some think of slowness, but is patient with ☒ [you], not [wanting] any to perish, but all to come to repentance.

REB: ....☒☒☒☒☒☒ [Here is something, dear friends, which you must not forget]: ☒ [in the Lord's sight] one day is like a thousand years, and a thousand years like one day. [It is] not that the Lord is slow [in

keeping] ⊠ his promise, as some ⊠ [suppose], but [that he] is patient
with ⊠ [you]. [It is] not [his will] ⊠⊠ that any should [be] lost,
but that all should come to repentance.

NAB: .... But ⊠⊠⊠⊠⊠⊠ [do not ignore this one fact,] beloved, that with
the Lord one day is like a thousand years, and a thousand years like
one day. The Lord [does not delay] ⊠⊠⊠ his promise, as some
regard delay, but [he] is patient [with you] ⊠⊠, not [wishing] that
any should perish but that all should come to repentance.

ANALYSIS: Verse 9 is one of the most misunderstood and misreported
verses in the NT. First, this is because of a failure to consider the
context in which it appears. Secondly, it is because the two governing
Greek words are misconstrued, sometimes deliberately, in an attempt
to establish universal salvation, or salvation through the will of man.
The governing word at the beginning of the chapter is Beloved. This group is
the US, those to whom God has granted life and godliness (1:3).
Another group is contrasted to the Beloved and may be referred to as
THEM. These appear throughout chapter 2, and in 3:3 through 3:7.
Verse 8 again is addressed to the Beloved (US), and verse 9 is a
continuation of that address, which does not end until verse 18.
Beloved is repeated in verse 14, and again in verse 17. That is the
context.

The two governing words of verse 9 are: *tinas* (any, #5100), and *boulemenos*
(purposing, willing with a purpose, #1014). *tinas*, from *tis*, is an
indefinite pronoun. In this verse it is accusative, masculine, and
plural. It can mean a certain group, some of a group. It could be used
of every person in the world IF all such persons were included in the
context. But if a more restricted group (such as the Beloved ones, the
US of this verse) is in view, it cannot mean every one of a more
comprehensive group (such as every person in the world). Therefore,
positively, "anyone" (NIV) is an incorrect translation, for there are
two groups in the context: (1) scoffers, unbelievers, and they are
opposed by the (2) Beloved, believers.

boulomenos, per Thayer's lexicon, is "of the will electing or choosing between
two or more things." It is a will of purpose, not a will of acquiescence,
much less a will of impotence. To translate the word here as wishing,
wanting, or any other word which leaves God restricted from His
eternal purposes, is not only incorrect, it is false on the face of it. If
God purposes that not one of His elect shall perish, then it is
insulting to Him to use a word that make Him out to be frustrated,
unable to fulfill His will in the life of any individual. If God's
purpose is that "the vessels of wrath fitted to destruction," (Rom.
9:22), the non-elect, should perish into everlasting fire, then who are
these new versionists that they presume to tell unbelievers that God is
not willing, wishing, wanting, for anyone of them to perish. Some
men seem willing to portray God as one with a double mind, being
torn between two desires, and thus frustrated. Oh Christian friends,
leave the frustrated god to those who have such a low opinion of the
ability of the true God to do His will in Heaven and on earth (Dan.
4:35).

These new versions are again teaching universal salvation. For if God is not willing for any person to perish, they most certainly will not perish. Much less is it true that the whole of mankind can thwart His will.

The popular new versions also take away the US at the beginning of verse 9, reporting that God's long-suffering (patience) is to you, rather than to US. They are relying on p72, Aleph, B, A, C, and a few late manuscripts. This change to you, instead of us, joined with their mistranslation of *tinas* as anyONE, solidifies their witness to universal salvation. It is the Beloved to whom God is long-suffering, and it is also the Beloved in view when it is said that *God is not willing for any to perish!*

And what is this to Christ? As it stands in the new versions, it frustrates the design of His sacrifice, making it out to be only a tentative salvation which is dependent on the will of man. And therefore it portrays Him as impotent, powerless to absolutely obtain the salvation of His elect people. And one that is powerless to achieve His purpose is certainly not God.

Hebrews 2:9

```
    3708    846         3956    5293                          1024  5100
9  ὁρῶμεν αὐτῷ τὰ πάντα ὑποτεταγμένα. τὸν δὲ βραχύ τι
   do we see to him   all things having been subjected. the (One) But  a little
   3844   32          1642          991        2424   1223
   παρ  ἀγγέλους ἠλαττωμένον βλέπομεν Ἰησοῦν, διὰ τό
   than   the angels having been made less we see,   Jesus, because of the
   3804       2288       1391       5092    4737        3704
   πάθημα τοῦ θανάτου δόξη καί τιμῇ ἐστεφανωμένον, ὅπως
   suffering   of death with glory and with honor having been crowned so as.
   5485     2316    5228  3956    1089        2288          4241    1063
10 χάριτι Θεοῦ ὑπέρ παντός γεύσηται θανάτου. ἔπρεπε γάρ
   by grace God's  for  every (son) He might taste of death. it was fitting For
```

KJV: ....But we see Jesus, who was made a little lower than the angels for the suffering of death, crowned with glory and honour; that he by the grace of God should taste death for every man.

LITV: ....But we do see Jesus, having been made less than the angels because of the suffering of death having been crowned with glory and with honor, so as by God's grace He might taste death for every [son].

MKJV: .....But we see Jesus, [who was] made a little lower than the angels for the suffering of death, crowned with glory and honor, that He by [the] grace of God should taste death for every [son].

NKJV: ..... But we see Jesus, who was made a little lower than the angels, for the suffering of death, crowned with glory and ☒ honor, that He, by the grace of God, might taste ☒ death for every[one]*

*NOTE: one is NOT in the Greek; the word is masculine, but it is governed by the context, therefore if any word is added it should be son (see vs. 10). Yet son, too, should be italicized. The addition of man in the Nestle is incorrect, not being either in the Greek or in the context. The benefits of the death of Christ are limited in the context to those persons who are sons, brothers, children of God. These words are taken from the 1982 edition of the NKJV. However, it should be known that there have been thousands of changes made in later printings without any notice to the reader that these have been made;

also a note on the copyright page of later editions should appear noting that it is a revision of the 1982 edition.

NIV: ....But we do see Jesus, [who was] made a little lower than the angels, [now] crowned with glory and honor because [he] ⊠ ⊠ suffered ⊠ death so that by the grace of God he might taste death for every[one].

NRSV: .....But we [do] see Jesus, who [for a little while] was made lower than the angels, [now] crowned with glory and honor because of the suffering of death, so that by the grace of God he might taste death for every[one].

NASB: .....But we do see [Him who] has been made [for little while] lower than the angels, [namely], Jesus, because of the suffering of death crowned with glory and honor, that by the grace of God He might taste death for every[one].

REB: ....[What] we do see [is] Jesus, [who for a short while] was made [subordinate to] ⊠⊠ the angels, crowned [now] with glory and honour because [he] ⊠ ⊠ suffered ⊠ death, so that by God's gracious [will], he ⊠⊠⊠ [should experience] death for all [mankind].

NAB: ....but we do see Jesus "crowned with glory and honor" because ⊠ ⊠ [he] suffered ⊠ death, [he who] "for a little while" was made "lower than the angels," that by the grace of God he might taste death for every [one].

ANALYSIS: The same new versions that would have Christ suffering for everyone (1 Peter 2:21); believing anyone (John 6:47); sacrificed for everyone (1 Cor. 5:7); bringing you (anyone, everyone) to God (1 Peter 3:18; dying for everyone (1 Peter 4:1); not willing/wanting/wishing that anyone should perish (2 Peter 3:9); making everyone an heir of God (Gal. 4:7), now here have Christ tasting death for everyone! (Hebrews 4:9). What is the Good News? If Christ did all that for every single person ("all mankind," per the REB), then there is no hell, no penalty for sin, in fact virtually no Bible left. This is another case where the context is violated by the new versionists. For when they have this opportunity of adding to what the original Greek says, they deliberately ignore the context in order to stick in their own view. And since they do NOT italicize, the reader of their versions are being deceived, and this without a clue that the 'translator' is giving his opinion, not God's words alone.

In the eighteenth century Unitarianism swept the professing Christian world. And that was one of the most ungodly of all centuries — until NOW. Once more we have noted 'conservative theologians' denying the existence of hell, translations like the NASB mistranslating so as to allow room for purgatory (Luke 1:72; Hebrews 9:27). By removing, or casting doubt on, dozens of verses that attest to the co-equal Godhead of Jesus Christ, these new versions are laying the groundwork for a New Age doctrine of Jesus that leaves Him unable to effect anything without the help of sinful men.

Galatians 4:7

1519   2588   5216   2896   5   3962   5820 3785
7   εἰς τὰς καρδίας ὑμῶν, κρᾶζον, Ἀββᾶ, ὁ πατήρ. ὥστε οὐκέτι
    into the hearts of you,   crying,   Abba,   Father! So as no more
    1487/1401   235   5207/1487 5207   2818   2316 1223
    εἰ δοῦλος, ἀλλ’ υἱός· εἰ δὲ υἱός, καὶ κληρονόμος Θεοῦ διὰ
    are you a slave, but a son; if and a son, also   an heir   of God by
    5547
    Χριστοῦ.
    Christ.

KJV: ....Wherefore thou art no more a servant, but a son; and if a son, then an heir of God through Christ.

MKJV: .....So that you are no longer a slave, but a son; and if a son, also an heir of God through Christ

NIV: ....So you are no longer a slave, but a son; and ☒ [since you are] a son, ☒ God [has made you] also an heir ☒ ☒

NASB: .....Therefore you are no longer a slave, but a son; and if a son, then an heir [through] ☒ God ☒ ☒

NRSV: .....Same as NASB.

REB: ....You are therefore no longer a slave but a son; and if a son, an heir ☒ ☒ [by [God's own act] ☒ ☒.

NAB: ....So you are no longer a slave but a ☒ [child], and if a ☒ [child], then also an heir, [through] God ☒☒☒.

ANALYSIS: Almost unanimously the Greek manuscripts testify that God's elect are made heirs through Christ. The corrupt mss. change this so that they are made heirs through God. In Rom. 8:17 we are told that we are joint-heirs with Christ. And since He always has the pre-eminence in all things, He first is heir through His eternal Sonship, and then we through Him. It should be unthinkable to imagine that we believers could receive any benefit without it coming through Christ. Yet these new versions seem quite willing to steal away those precious words through Christ in this verse. Why? Why this officious shortening of the Scriptures simply because of a few man-made, man-oriented rules that the critics have made up for their own purposes? This business of which words are God-breathed words is not child's play, but serious business. We all shall be judged by them: "the word that I have spoken, the same shall judge him in the last day (John 12:48).

EVIDENCE: Once more our new versionists have put their trust in only four Egyptian mss., p46, Aleph, A, B. And on the basis of these four corrupted, error-filled, omission-filled mss., are we to agree that God's elect are NOT made heirs through Christ? Never!

100

13 δικαίως καὶ εὐσεβῶς ζήσωμεν ἐν τῷ νῦν αἰῶνι, προσδεχό-
righteously and godly we might live in the present age. expecting
μενοι τὴν μακαρίαν ἐλπίδα καὶ ἐπιφάνειαν τῆς δόξης τοῦ
the blessed hope and appearance of the glory of the
14 μεγάλου Θεοῦ καὶ σωτῆρος ἡμῶν Ἰησοῦ Χριστοῦ, ὃς ἔδωκεν
great God and Savior of us, Jesus Christ, who gave
ἑαυτὸν ὑπὲρ ἡμῶν, ἵνα λυτρώσηται ἡμᾶς ἀπὸ πάσης
Himself on behalf of us, that He might redeem us from all
ἀνομίας, καὶ καθαρίσῃ ἑαυτῷ λαὸν περιούσιον, ζηλωτὴν
iniquity, and cleanse for Himself a people special, zealous
καλῶν ἔργων,
of good works.

KJV: ....Looking for that blessed hope, and the glorious appearing of the great God and our Saviour Jesus Christ; Who gave himself for us, that he might redeem us from all iniquity, and purify unto himself a peculiar people, zealous of good works.

MKJV: .....looking for the blessed hope, and the glorious appearance of our great God and Savior Jesus Christ, who gave Himself for us that He might redeem us from all iniquity and purify to Himself a special people, zealous of good works.

NIV: ....looking forward to the [happy fulfillment of our] ☒ hope ☒ ☒ ☒ ☒ ☒ [when the splendour] of [our] great God and Saviour Christ Jesus [will appear]. [He it is] who ☒ [sacrificed] himself for us, to set us free from all wickedness and [to make us his own] ☒☒☒☒☒ people, [pure and eager to do] ☒☒ good.☒

NASB: .....looking for the blessed hope and the appearing of the glory of our great God and Savior, Christ Jesus, who gave Himself for us, that He might redeem us from [every lawless deed] ☒☒ and purify for Himself a ☒ people [for His own possession], zealous for good deeds.

NRSV: .....☒ ☒ ☒ [while we wait] for the blessed hope and the manifestation of the glory of our great God and Savior Jesus Christ. [He it is] who gave himself for us that he might redeem us from all iniquity and purify for himself a ☒ people [of his own] who are zealous for good deeds.

REB: ....☒ ☒ [while we wait] for the blessed hope — the glorious [appearing] of our great God and Savior, Jesus Christ, who gave himself for us to redeem us from all wickedness and to purify for himself a ☒ people [that are his own], [eager to do what is] ☒☒ good.

NAB: ....☒ ☒ [as we await] the blessed hope, ☒ the appearance of the glory of the great God and [of our] Savior Jesus Christ, who gave himself for us ☒ ☒ ☒ to deliver us from all lawlessness and to cleanse for himself a people [of his own], eager [to do what is] good.

NOTE the many words which do not translate the Greek. The NIV has 50 English words to express the 35 Greek words in these two verses. But only 27 of those 50 express the Greek they were supposed to be translating, and 23 of the NIV words do not reflect the Greek. That is a 46% error rate, not counting the words they did not translate at all. Then look at the NAB where they put two words in between God and Savior (of our), as if there were a distinction between God and our Savior. And they all feel confident in changing the grammatical construction of the God-breathed words at one place or another.

ANALYSIS: But they may say, "We do not hold back from giving Christ the title of God, as you will see if you will look at John 20:28, Titus 2:13, and 2 Peter 1:1." One might answer with a question: "If your favorite manuscripts, B, or Aleph, or only D, did not have the word God in those passages, would you still have them in your version?" The question here is this: Is Jesus Christ God because Codices B, Aleph, and D say so? Or, if B, Aleph, and D do not say that Jesus Christ is God at any place, should the reference to God be omitted from a new version? Should we not consider whether in the first four centuries there was not a feverish, perverted attempt to delete, or to change, references which testified to Christ's Godhood? Do not the gospel and epistles of John answer that question, for as he was borne along by the Holy Spirit of God, John wrote more fully to testify that Jesus Christ is God. "And we are in Him that is true, in His Son Jesus Christ; this is the true God, and the everlasting life" (1 John 5:20).

Shall the new versions be praised because at some places they still acknowledge Christ as God, and at the same time silently acquiesce in the altering of Scriptures so that they do not testify that Christ is God?

Among men, those who persist may be entitled to their opinion, saying that the Egyptian manuscripts are the major arbiters of what is, and what is not, Scripture. But it is ONLY an opinion, and by no means a proven fact. Before the judgment seat of Christ on that Day, if not before, we are convinced that they will see the error in their judgments.

Isaiah 6:3, 5

3 פָּנָיו וּבִשְׁתַּיִם יְכַסֶּה רַגְלָיו וּבִשְׁתַּיִם יְעוֹפֵף : וְקָרָא זֶה
this And .flew he with and his he with and his .face
cried two feet two

אֶל־זֶה וְאָמַר קָדוֹשׁ ׀ קָדוֹשׁ קָדוֹשׁ יְהוָה צְבָאוֹת מְלֹא
(is) ;hosts Jehovah (is) holy ,holy ,Holy ,said and this to
full of

4 כָל־הָאָרֶץ כְּבוֹדוֹ : וַיָּנֻעוּ אַמּוֹת הַסִּפִּים מִקּוֹל הַקּוֹרֵא
one the the from the the And His (of) the all
called who of voice threshold of posts shook glory earth

5 וְהַבַּיִת יִמָּלֵא עָשָׁן : וָאֹמַר אוֹי־לִי כִי־נִדְמֵיתִי כִי אִישׁ טְמֵא־
unclean a for am I for to Woe I Then .smoke was the and
of man ,off cut ,me said with filled house

שְׂפָתַיִם אָנֹכִי וּבְתוֹךְ עַם־טְמֵא שְׂפָתַיִם אָנֹכִי יֹשֵׁב כִי אֶת־
for ,live I lips unclean a and .(am) I lips
of people amongst

6 הַמֶּלֶךְ יְהוָה צְבָאוֹת רָאוּ עֵינָי : וַיָּעָף אֵלַי אֶחָד מִן־הַשְּׂרָפִים
the of one to Then my have ,hosts Jehovah the
seraphim me flew .eyes seen of ,King

KJV: ....And one cried unto another, and said, Holy, holy, holy, [is] the LORD of hosts: the whole earth [is] full of his glory. Then said I, Woe [is] me! for I am undone; because I [am] a man of unclean lips, and I dwell in the midst of a people of unclean lips: for mine eyes have seen the King, the LORD of hosts.

MKJV: .....And one cried to another, and said, Holy, holy, holy, [is] the LORD (Jehovah) of hosts; the whole earth [is] full [of] His glory . . . . Then I said, Woe is me! For I am undone; for I [am] a man of unclean lips, and I dwell in the midst of a people of unclean lips; for my eyes have seen the King, Jehovah.

NIV: ....And [they were] calling to one another. Holy, holy, holy [is] the LORD [Almighty]; the whole earth [is] full [of] his glory . . . . ⊠ Woe is me! I cried, ⊠⊠⊠⊠⊠ I am a man of unclean lips, and I live among a people of unclean lips, and my eyes have seen the King, the LORD [Almighty].

The NASB, NRSV, REB, NAB agree with the MKJV.

ANALYSIS: This Holy One, the LORD, in the original Hebrew is **Jehovah of hosts.** And in John 12:41, we see that Isaiah is speaking of the Messiah, Christ Jesus, who is Jehovah of hosts:

```
      2588   2443/3361 1492          3788              3539
41  καρδίαν· ἵνα μὴ ἴδωσι τοῖς ὀφθαλμοῖς, καὶ νοήσωσι τῇ
    heart,  that not they might see with the eyes,  and  understand with
    2588                  2390  846     5023  2036 the
    καρδίᾳ, καὶ ἐπιστραφῶσι, καὶ ἰάσωμαι αὐτούς. ταῦτα εἶπεν
    heart,  and  be converted,  and I should heal them. These things said
    2268   3753/1492   1391 848        2980   4012  846
    Ἡσαΐας, ὅτε εἶδε τὴν δόξαν αὐτοῦ, καὶ ἐλάλησε περὶ αὐτοῦ.
    Isaiah  when he saw the glory  of Him,  and  spoke  about  Him.
```

KJV: .... These things said Esaias, when he saw his glory, and spake of him.

MKJV: ..... Isaiah said these things when He saw His glory and spoke of Him.

All versions agree on this verse.

ANALYSIS: Isaiah said, "My eyes have seen the King, Jehovah." John testifies
that the Person Isaiah saw was Christ (see vs. 38). Therefore, the One
who is being saluted with those pregnant words, "Holy, holy, holy!" was
both Jehovah, and at the same time God the Son. And the same words
are addressed to Christ in Rev. 4:8: "Holy, holy, holy, Lord God, the
Almighty, [who] was, and is, and [is] coming."

Can Jehovah, the Lord God Almighty, be a created Being? Let no one dare to
say it!

Isaiah 43:14, 15

KJV: .... Thus saith the LORD, your redeemer, the Holy One of Israel; . . . I [am]
the LORD, your Holy One, the creator of Israel, your King.

MKJV: ..... So says the LORD (Jehovah), your Redeemer, the Holy One of Israel .
. . I [am] the LORD (Jehovah), your Holy One, the Creator of Israel,
your King.

NIV: .... ☒ [This is what] the LORD says—your Redeemer, the Holy One of
Israel . . . I am the LORD, your Holy One, Israel's Creator, your King.

The NASB, NRSV, REB, the same.

ANALYSIS: There you have it all. Keep in mind that when these versions print
LORD in capitals, the Hebrew says Jehovah. Isaiah's Immanuel is
Jehovah, the great Redeemer, the Holy One, the Creator, and King.
With such things being said in the OT, how can we allow without
vigorous protest any of the critics or the new versionists to issue an
uncertain sound from their trumpets, one verse testifying that Jesus is
God, and another verse taking it all away from Him?

PERFECTION

1 John 3:5

```
     458    4160        266   2076       458          1492
5  ἀνομίαν ποιεῖ· καὶ ἡ ἁμαρτία ἐστὶν ἡ ἀνομία. καὶ οἴδατε ὅτι
   lawlessness does; and    sin    is    lawlessness. And you know that
     1565   5319      2443       266       2257   142      266
   ἐκεῖνος ἐφανερώθη, ἵνα τὰς ἁμαρτίας ἡμῶν ἄρῃ· καὶ ἁμαρτία
   that (One) was revealed that the   sins    of us He might bear, and  sin
     1722/ 846/3756/2076/3956  1722/846    3306  3756  264      3956
6  ἐν αὐτῷ οὐκ ἐστι. πᾶς ὁ ἐν αὐτῷ μένων οὐχ ἁμαρτάνει· πᾶς
   in   Him   not  is. Everyone in Him remaining not    sins;  everyone
```

KJV: ....And ye know that he was manifested to take away our sins; and in him is no sin.

MKJV: .....And you know that He was revealed that he might bear our sins, and in Him is no sin.

ERV: ....⊠ You know that ⊠ ⊠ ⊠ ⊠ ⊠ ⊠ ⊠ ⊠ [Christ came to take away people's] sins. ⊠ [There] is no sin in [Christ].

NIV: ....But you know that he appeared so that he might take away our sins ⊠ ⊠ ⊠ ⊠ ⊠ ⊠.

NASB: .....And you know that He appeared in order to take away ⊠⊠ sins; and to Him there is no sin.

NRSV: .....⊠ You know that he was revealed to take away ⊠⊠ sins, and in him is no sin.

REB: ....⊠ You know that [Christ] appeared in order to take away ⊠⊠ sins, and in him there is no sin.

NAB: ....⊠ You know that he was revealed to take away ⊠⊠ sins, and in him there is no sin.

Note that every version has the words "in him is no sin" EXCEPT the NIV. You would think that they had some very heavy and compelling evidence which encourages them to remove this affirmation of the sinlessness of Christ. But they do not.

ANALYSIS: All the new versions except KJV, LITV, MKJV, NKJV and NIV again have taken away this plain statement that Christ was revealed in order to take away our sins. Surely someone went through Codex B, or its ancestor, eliminating our hope that Christ suffered and died for the sins of a specific group of people, the elect. For only A and B of the Greek manuscripts can be cited as witnesses that in this verse Christ DID NOT appear to take away our sins. Pity the poor souls who depend on Codices A and B to give them hope of salvation in Christ Jesus. For there is no hope without His complete satisfaction for sins. Codex B blights this hope throughout the New Testament Scriptures as we have seen in this short study.

_{1188 302 5407   1777   2071   2920 1473   3004 5213}
22 δ' ἂν φονεύσῃ, ἔνοχος ἔσται τῇ κρίσει· ἐγὼ δὲ λέγω ὑμίν
_{and ever murders, liable shall be to the Judgment. I But say to you}
_{3754 3956   3710   80   848   1500 1777 2071}
ὅτι πᾶς ὁ ὀργιζόμενος τῷ ἀδελφῷ αὐτοῦ εἰκῆ ἔνοχος ἔσται
_{that each who is angry with the brother of him without liable shall be}
_{2920 3739 .302 2036   80   945   4469   1777}
τῇ κρίσει· ὃς δ' ἂν εἴπῃ τῷ ἀδελφῷ αὐτου, Ρακά, ἔνοχος
_{to the Judgment. who and ever says to brother of him, Raca, liable}

KJV: ....But I say unto you, That whosoever is angry with his brother **without a cause** shall be in danger of the judgment:

MKJV: .....But I say to you that whoever is angry with his brother **without a cause** shall be liable to the judgment.

ERV: ....But I [tell] ☒ ☒ you, [don't be] ☒ ☒ angry with [another person. Every person is your brother. If you] are angry ☒ ☒ ☒ [with other people, you] will be ☒ ☒ ☒ ☒ [judged].

NIV: ....But I [tell] you that anyone who is angry with his brother ☒ ☒ ☒ will be subject to ☒ judgment.

NASB: .....But I say to you that everyone who is angry with his brother ☒ ☒ ☒ shall be [guilty before the court].

NRSV: .....But I say to you that if you are angry with a brother ☒ ☒ ☒ [or a sister], you will be liable to judgment;

REB: ....But [what] I [tell] you [is this]: Anyone who ☒☒ [nurses anger] [against] ☒ his brother ☒☒☒☒☒☒ [must be brought to justice].

NAB: ....But I say to you, whoever is angry with his brother ☒ ☒ ☒ will be liable to judgment.

CEV: ....But I ☒ ☒ ☒ ☒ ☒ ☒ [promise you if you are] angry with ☒☒ [someone, you will have to stand trial] ☒☒☒☒☒☒.

ANALYSIS: The NIV, NASB, NRSV, REB, NAB, GNB, ERV, JWV all leave out the translation of the one key word, *eike*, which translated means "**without a cause.**" What difference does it make? They say that whoever is angry will be subject to judgment (the NASB, ERV, CEV mistranslate the word meaning judgment). But the Lord Jesus was angry on several occasions. Who is it that will stand in judgment over Him? Who dares to say that He is liable to judgment? And if one is liable to judgment, it cannot mean anything else but that that one is a sinner. By leaving out this key word, the modern versionists are making Jesus a sinner, liable to judgment. Do they not care to protect Him from such a charge?

What is the evidence? In his book, *The Identity of the New Testament Text*, Wilbur N. Pickering gives us the following:

On the basis of two Egyptian uncial MSS., B and Aleph, one papyrus (p[67]) and 2 cursives (01*, 045), these men would have us to believe that God contradicted Himself in the Bible, and even worse, that since Jesus was angry on several occasions, the new versions would make Jesus liable to the Judgment, a sinner, because only sinners are liable to the Judgment. Opposing the Egyptian manuscripts are all others, including D, E, K, L, M, S, V, W, 037, 038, 041, 042, 0233, f[1,13], 33, Italian, Syriac and Coptic versions." Morris incorrectly claims D, K, and L omit. The Peshitto Syriac Version (c. 150 A.D.), not only has the word, but has the very Greek word **eike** in it.

The words **without a cause** limit the statement to those who are angry **without a cause**, while permitting anger when there is cause, in God's cause. Without this one little word (*eike*), the verse would say that whoever is angry is liable to the Judgment. Where is the contradiction? God is said to be angry. Jesus, Moses, David, and other key figures were said to be angry. And of these only Moses is judged wrong, and that because he disobeyed a specific command. Eph. 4:26 does not prohibit anger.

Note that the latest versions, ERV, CEV and REB almost completely rewrite this verse. The ERV has 25 words, 17 of which are their words, not God's words. The CEV has 16 words, but only 4 of them translate what God wrote. The REB has 19 words, 11 of which are not translations of the Greek they chose to translate.

This is just another instance where the modern versions have statements that contradict what they say elsewhere, and also it might be noted that they contradict each other consistently.

Burgon lists 30 patristic fathers who quoted the verse with **eike**, including Irenaeus, Cyprian, and Justin Martyr. He pins the blame on Origen, a Gnostic (c. 200 A.D.) who did not believe that Jesus was God. At one place Origen quotes the verse with **eike**. Even when he says it ought to be omitted, it proves that he had a manuscript which included **eike**, a manuscript older than Origen's time. See *Unholy Hands on the Bible*, Vol. I, p. G-60 (also UH II, p. 331, 560) for the full evidence.

DID JESUS LIE TO HIS BROTHERS?

John 7:8

```
   2041  848   4190   2076  5210   306    1519        1859
8 τὰ ἔργα αὐτοῦ πονηρά ἐστιν. ὑμεῖς ἀνάβητε εἰς τὴν ἑορτὴν
the works  of it    evil     are.    You   go up    to      feast
   5026  1473  3768   305    1519         1859     5026  3764
  ταύτην· ἐγὼ οὔπω ἀναβαίνω εἰς τὴν ἑορτὴν ταύτην, ὅτι ὁ
  this;   I   not yet am going to  -    feast   this, because
   2540   1899 3768    4137        5023       2036   846
9 καιρὸς ὁ ἐμὸς οὔπω πεπλήρωται. ταῦτα δὲ εἰπὼν αὐτοῖς,
  time    My   not yet has been fulfilled. these things And saying to them.
```

Besides the instance of an omitted word making Jesus to be a sinner liable to the Judgment (Matt. 5:22), there is another verse where six of the new versions make Jesus to be a liar. In John 7:8, in the NASB, NRSV, REB, NAB, GNB, CEV by rejecting the little word yet (*ouro* - #3768), Jesus is reported as telling a lie:

KJV: ....Go ye up unto this feast: I go not up yet unto this feast; for my time is not yet full come.

MKJV: .....You go up to this feast; I am not yet going up to this feast, for My time is not yet fulfilled.

NIV: ....You go to the Feast. I am not yet going up to this Feast, because for [me the right] ☒ time [has] not ☒ [come].

NRSV: .....☒ Go up to ☒ the festival [yourselves]. I am not ☒ going to this festival; for my time is not ☒ [fully come]

NASB: .....You go up to the feast [yourselves]; I [do] not ☒ go up to this feast because My time has not yet [fully come].

REB: ....☒ Go up to the festival [yourselves]. I am not ☒ going up to this festival, because ☒ [the right] time has not yet [come].

NAB: ....You go up to the feast. I am not ☒ going up to this feast because my time has not yet been fulfilled.

The NASB, NRSV, REB, NAB, GNB, CEV, and JWV all also have Jesus saying flatly: 'I am not going up to this feast.' By leaving out the word yet these versions make Jesus to tell a lie, as is proven by the fact that shortly thereafter He did go up to the feast.

On what compelling evidence do these new versions base the omission of this very important word yet? How much evidence must they have to make them willing to convict Jesus of lying to His brothers. They have ONLY Aleph, D, and K, with some Latin and Syriac copies. But notice this: Codex B, their idol manuscript DOES HAVE yet! And that is probably the only reason the NIV has "yet" in their version. Add in 2,000 or more other Greek manuscripts, then try to balance Aleph, D, and K against B, the other uncials and the cursives, literally thousands of manuscripts, reporting correctly that Jesus did not lie.

This is an example of what Gordon Clark wrote: "The flaws in the revised text [of the new versions - Ed.] are not incidental and unintentional lapses. They are the result of a pervasive and controlling methodology" (P. 24, *Logical Criticisms of Textual Criticism*, Jefferson, MD: Trinity Foundation). In other words, there is method in the madness of the modern critics and new versionists. Do they not seem to be much more concerned with enhancing their own reputations, and in following their own self-concocted rules, than they are concerned with the reputation of Jesus Christ, our God and Savior?

VIRGIN BIRTH

Matthew 1:25

```
        3880        1135      848     3756  1097    846
κal  παρέλαβε  τὴν  γυναῖκα  αὐτοῦ,  καὶ  οὐκ  ἐγίνωσκεν  αὐτὴν
and  took    (as) the  wife    of him   and  not  did know    her
        2193/3739/5088   5207   848            4416           2564
25  ἕως  οὗ  ἔτεκε  τὸν  υἱὸν  αὐτῆς  τὸν  πρωτότοκον·  καὶ  ἐκάλεσε
    until  she bore the  son  of her,  the    firstborn.    And he called
        3686       848    2424
    τὸ  ὄνομα  αὐτοῦ  ᾿ΙΗΣΟΥΝ.
    the  name  of Him,    JESUS.
```

KJV: ....And knew her not till she had brought forth her **firstborn** son: and he called his name JESUS.

MKJV: .....and did not know her until she bore her son, the **firstborn**. And he called His name Jesus.

ERV: ....But ☒☒☒ [Joseph had no sexual union with Mary] until she gave birth to [the] ☒ son, ☒ ☒. And ☒ [Joseph] named [the son] ☒☒ Jesus.

NIV: ....But ☒ [he had no union with] her ☒ until she gave birth to ☒ [a] son, ☒ ☒. And he ☒ [gave him the] ☒ name [of] Jesus.

NASB: .....and ☒ [kept] her ☒ [a virgin] until she gave birth to ☒ ☒, ☒ ☒ [a] Son, and he called His name Jesus.

NRSV: .....but ☒ [had no marital relations with] ☒ her ☒ until she had borne ☒ ☒, ☒ ☒ [a] son]; and he named him Jesus.

REB: ....but ☒ [had no intercourse with] ☒ her until [her] ☒☒☒ son [was born] ☒☒☒. And he named ☒ [the child] Jesus.

GNB: ......But [he had no sexual relations with her before] ☒☒☒☒ she gave birth to her son ☒☒. And [Joseph] ☒ named [him] ☒☒ Jesus.

CEV: ....But [they did not live together before] her ☒☒☒☒☒☒☒ [baby was born]. Then [Joseph] named [him] ☒☒ Jesus.

ANALYSIS: Was Jesus Mary's **firstborn** Son? Except for the KJV, MKJV, LITV, and NKJV you would not know that Jesus was the **firstborn** from this verse. What mound of evidence must have been piled up against "**firstborn**" that it must be excluded from this verse! Here is the evidence:

"**firstborn** son" is the reading of every manuscript except the following Egyptian MSS.: Aleph, B, Z, f², 33. So well attested is **firstborn** that the Greek, Latin, and Syriac churches all unanimously agree on it, even the Vulgate has it, in spite of their doctrine of the perpetual virginity of Mary. The dropping of **firstborn** from Aleph and B is a corruption reflecting the Gnostic-dominated Egyptians who desired to remove any word which would imply the deity of Jesus Christ. So they read "a son" as if His was only a common birth. But here even Codex W, another Egyptian MS. of the fourth or fifth century has **firstborn** in Matthew. The wilfully blind critics would have us believe that a word (**firstborn**) has been sinfully added to every Greek, Syriac, and Latin manuscript in all places in the habitable world. At the same time they would have us believe that God has chosen the heretics of Egypt, Gnostic and Arian, to preserve His precious Word.

B and Aleph, Nestle/UBS, the Gnostics notwithstanding, Jesus was the **firstborn** son of Mary, and the **firstborn** Son of God! (John 1:18; Luke 2:7).

32 $\overset{602}{\text{ἀποκάλυψιν}}$ $\overset{1484}{\text{ἐθνῶν.}}$ $\overset{1391}{\text{καὶ}}$ $\overset{2992}{\text{δόξαν}}$ $\overset{4875}{\text{λαοῦ}}$ $\overset{2474}{\text{σου}}$ $\overset{2258}{\text{ἰσραήλ.}}$ $\overset{2258}{\text{καὶ ἦν}}$
revelation (to the) nations, and a glory of people of You Israel. And was

33 $\overset{2501}{\text{Ἰωσὴφ}}$ $\overset{3384}{\text{καὶ}}$ $\overset{848}{\text{ἡ}}$ $\overset{2296}{\text{μήτηρ}}$ $\overset{1909}{\text{αὐτοῦ}}$ $\overset{2980}{\text{θαυμάζοντες}}$ $\overset{}{\text{ἐπὶ}}$ $\overset{}{\text{τοῖς λαλου-}}$
Joseph and the mother of Him marveling at the things being

34 $\overset{4012}{\text{μένοις}}$ $\overset{846}{\text{περὶ}}$ $\overset{}{\text{αὐτοῦ.}}$ $\overset{2127}{\text{καὶ}}$ $\overset{846}{\text{εὐλόγησεν}}$ $\overset{4826}{\text{αὐτοὺς}}$ $\overset{}{\text{Σιμεών,}}$ $\overset{2036}{\text{καὶ εἶπε}}$
said about Him. And blessed them Simeon, and said

KJV: ....And Joseph and his mother marvelled at those things which were spoken of him.

MKJV: .....And Joseph was marveling, also His mother, at the things being said about Him.

ERV: .... ☒ [Jesus' father] ☒ and ☒ mother [were] amazed at ☒☒☒☒ [what Simeon] said about him.

NIV: ....☒☒ [The child's father] and ☒ mother marveled at ☒☒☒ [what] was said about him.

NASB: .....And ☒ [His father] and ☒ mother were amazed at the things which were being said about Him.

NRSV: .....And ☒ [the child's father] and ☒ mother were amazed at ☒ ☒ [what was] being said about him.

REB: ....And [the child's father] ☒ and ☒ mother were [full of wonder] at ☒ ☒ [what was] being said about him.

NAB: ....☒ [The child's father] and ☒ mother were amazed at ☒ ☒ [what] was said about him.

CEV: ....☒☒☒☒☒☒☒☒☒ [The child's parents were surprised at what Simeon had] said.

Not one word of the CEV's 'translation' translates the Greek!

The NASB, REB, NRSV, GNB, NAB, JWV all identify Joseph as the father of Jesus. Search the commentaries of the past 100 years, and you can hardly find a single commentator who does not favor 'his father and mother' here. Once again our learned gentlemen have been careless of the reputation of Jesus. It has come to the point where some 'theologians' are boldly telling seminarians that Jesus possibly was the son of a barbarian soldier.

EVIDENCE: Again it is the Egyptian mss. Aleph, B, D, W, and L. How easy it is to imagine a Gnostic scribe deliberately and gleefully changing Joseph to father, thereby contradicting the marvelous story of Luke 1 which names God the Holy Spirit as the father of Jesus IN EVERY ONE of these same versions.

A SUMMARY OF THE EVIDENCE PRESENTED ABOVE

Having surveyed some 110 verses of the Scriptures which touch on the essential Godhood of Jesus Christ, and having presented at one place or another the words of 12 different new versions in order to show their treatment of the deity of Christ, a summary of the findings seems to be an appropriate ending to this discussion.

By now proof of the twenty-one basic findings mentioned at the beginning of this book should have been amply presented. In addition a summary of the various versions might include the following:

Of the new versions, the KJV, LITV, MKJV, NKJV (except in Heb. 2:9) versions have been found to faithfully retain and present Christ as a co-equal Person in the Trinity, one in essence with God the Father and God the Holy Spirit. All words added for sense in those versions are italicized, and there is no pattern of adding words which will affect the interpretation of any of these verses. The LITV translations may be seen under the Hebrew and Greek words which we have drawn from *The Interlinear Hebrew-Greek-English Bible*. Because the KJV, MKJV, and NKJV very often read the same, in most cases only the KJV and MKJV is used for a comparison with the other new versions.

The ERV, CEV versions are the newest releases. They are included to show the trend toward an almost complete rewriting of the Scriptures. This is a trend that started with the NIV's addition of 100,000+ man-breathed words, and their decision not to translate thousands of the original words. Translators appear to be infected with the virus of pride, seeing themselves as the saviors of the age, feeling quite competent to improve on the God-breathed words that were inscripturated by God the Holy Spirit through the prophets and apostles. There is an assumption that there is no need to show any scriptural authority for their decision to cast out God-breathed words, and to cast in words formulated in their own minds, without "being borne along by the Holy Spirit" (2 Pet. 1:21). This dependence on the ability of the 'independent mind' to discern among diverse manuscripts 'the ring of truth' is not a new phenomenon. The most prominent and noted member of this proud society must be Origen (c. 185 - c. 254 A.D.), the Gnostic intellectual who fancied himself the final authority on what is, and what is not true Scripture. Many were the wounds in the text left behind by Origen. But before and after Origen, the faithful churches were guided by God the Spirit to guard the Deposit, casting aside adulterated manuscripts, and reproducing faithful ones. After four centuries of turmoil, the Greek text as a whole came to be reproduced in the same words, with only minor differences.

However, the Latin text was not purified to the same extent, retaining many of the heretical additions and omissions of the first centuries. When Jerome, an admirer of Origen, consolidated the Latin text by producing the Vulgate (384 - 404 A.D.), he apparently used Greek mss. of the Origenic variety, later typified by Codices B and Aleph, for the NT.

111

After Erasmus produced what is essentially now called the Received Text in 1516, and Stephanas printed it in 1550, the predominance of this Greek text was not seriously threatened until the nineteenth century. Westcott and Hort and their hand-picked cronies dominated the revision committee which produced the Revised Version. Then, in 1880, for the first time since the early centuries, many of the heresies of the early centuries, mainly those of the Gnostics, were reinserted into a Greek 'text' (essentially that of Westcott and Hort). It is the most deadly of the corruptions introduced to attack the Godhood of Christ that we have considered in this book.

In this century the ARV, RSV, GNB, NASB, NEB, NIV, NRSV, REB, NAB, CEV, and a host of other versions have increasingly changed what they call the Holy Bible into something else. As time progressed, boldness increased. This slipping over the line was accelerated by the NIV. In that version can be found not only the omissions of the Egyptian mss., but the casting out of what they called **excess words** (in their pamphlet entitled *The Story of the New International Bible*).' And these so-called 'excess words' include tens of thousands of words which were in the original languages they chose to translate. In some verses, less than 20% of the original Greek is represented by the English words in the NIV (see Acts 27:37, where the number 276 is the only true translation of that verse in the NIV). In the historical reporting of Jael and Sisera, the NIV left untranslated dozens of words (Judges 4:17; 5:6). And their additions of words of their own formulation must exceed 100,000 of the 730,000 words in the NIV. But all of the above named new versions add and subtract words, with only the NASB of the later new versions using italics as a means of identifying added words. And the NASB has added thousands of words **without** italicizing them. Of the latest new versions based on the Alexandrian, Egyptian manuscripts, the NAB sticks closer to the Nestle[26]/UBS[3] Greek they are translating, and the REB, ERV, CEV go further even than the NIV in producing a commentary rather than a translation.

Although the Alexandrian-based manuscripts and versions above do not always walk in lockstep, it has been demonstrated that they most often unite in presenting to the public those verses which rob Christ of His divine attributes, the verses that testify to His co-equal, essential Godhood.

SCRIPTURES TO MEDITATE UPON

When deciding whether one may rest one's soul on one of the new versions, carefully consider whether they meet the following tests (Scriptures from *The Literal Translation of the Bible*):

"Man shall not live by bread alone, but by every word having proceeded through the mouth of God" (Matthew 4:4, Luke 4:4).

"Do you not err because of this, not knowing the Scriptures, nor the power of God?" (Mark 12:24).

"Then faith [is] of hearing, and hearing through a word of God" (Romans 10:17).

"But we have renounced the hidden things of shame, not walking in craftiness, nor adulterating the Word of God" (2 Corinthians 4:2).

"And because of this we give thanks to God without ceasing, that having received [the] word of hearing from us, you welcomed [it as] of God, not [as] a word of men, but as it is, truly [the] Word of God, which also works in you, the [ones] believing" (1 Thessalonians 2:13).

"For the Word of God [is] living, and powerfully working, and sharper than every two-mouthed sword, and piercing as far as [the] division of both soul and spirit, of both joints and of marrows, and able to judge of thoughts and intentions of a heart" (Hebrews 4:12).

Pray that the Holy Spirit of Truth will "guide you into all truth" (John 16:13), with the words He has preserved through centuries, and which may be found in a consensus of the vast majority of the Hebrew and Greek manuscripts now known to us. Though these thousands of manuscripts have their individuality, differing in minor ways, with the exception of the Egyptian manuscripts, they with one accord testify to the Godhood of Jesus, He being one in essence with God the Father and God the Holy Spirit.